Go Through the Gates

Embrace Your Time in the Presence of God

Go Through the Gates

Embrace Your Time in the Presence of God

Maxine Cedergreen

© Copyright 1995 — Maxine Cedergreen

All rights reserved. This book is protected under the copyright laws of the United States of America. This book may not be copied or reprinted for commercial gain or profit. Short quotations or occasional page copying for personal or group study is permitted and encouraged. Permission will be granted upon request. Unless otherwise identified, Scripture quotations are taken from the New American Standard of the Bible, © 1960, 1962, 1963, 1968, 1971, 1972, 1973, 1975, 1977 by The Lockman Foundation. Other Scripture quotations are from The Living Bible (TLB) and the King James Version (KJV). Emphasis within Scripture is the author's own.

Take note that the name satan and related names are not capitalized. We choose not to acknowledge him, even to the point of violating grammatical rules.

Companion Press
P.O. Box 310
Shippensburg, PA 17257-0310

"Good Stewards of the
Manifold Grace of God"

ISBN 1-56043-649-2

For Worldwide Distribution
Printed in the U.S.A.

Dedication

To my husband Eldon, a building
contractor who is well acquainted with the
carpenter from Nazareth.

Contents

	Preface	ix
	Introduction	xi
Chapter 1	The Garden Gate	1
Chapter 2	The Floodgates of the Sky	11
Chapter 3	Gate of God	17
Chapter 4	Gate of Sodom	21
Chapter 5	Gate of Heaven	31
Chapter 6	Gate to the Camp	43
Chapter 7	Gate of Jericho	53
Chapter 8	The Gates of Eckron	67
Chapter 9	Outside the Gate	83
Chapter 10	The Narrow Gate	99
Chapter 11	Gates of Righteousness	115
Chapter 12	Gates of Zion	127

Preface

This unusual book, written in a relaxed, easy-to-read style, is designed for the layman. But make no mistake, for the message, while somewhat veiled at the beginning, is nevertheless profound. It penetrates slowly and deeply as the Holy Spirit personally unlocks the hidden meanings to each reader.

The author's clear lack of certified credentials is overridden by her conscientious accounting of Scripture and adherence to its original intent and by her absolute reliance on the Holy Spirit. The life within these parallel studies of Old Testament stories speaks for itself candidly, uniquely, and without assistance.

There are three levels of understanding within the dimension of this book. The brand new believer will receive a good foundational background concerning God's plan. The more mature student will pick up on some of the types and symbols as he "discovers" truths that were hidden to him before. With his eagle eye, the committed seeker of truth will be alert to the sprinkling of fresh revelation knowledge. His own renewed mind, fine-tuned to the Word by the Holy Spirit, will meditate upon each concept, judge it against God's truth, and proceed to new ground. He will be challenged to unravel all the layers within, allowing God to speak freely to him.

The first reading of this book should be relaxed and enjoyable. This is not a textbook to study or memorize; but rather, it is a ticket for an exciting chariot ride that takes you to that "secret place" in God.

As a matter of fact, the chariot driver will be glad to drop you at the gate that leads directly to the throne room, where the King is waiting for you.

Foreword

People from around the world will come on pilgrimages and pour into Jerusalem from many foreign cities to attend these celebrations. People will write to their friends in other cities and say, "Let's go to Jerusalem to ask the Lord to bless us, and be merciful to us. I'm going! Please come with me. Let's go now!" (Zechariah 8:20-21 TLB)

Answering the phone, I heard our daughter's voice on the other end from her home in a distant city. "We're going to Jerusalem. Come, go with us," she suggested. At first I thought she was joking, but she wasn't. So within a few short weeks the four of us were high above Italy on a 747 headed for Israel.

The beginnings of this book were brooding in me during the press of the pilgrimage. Scriptures surfaced momentarily; then like vapors they were gone and forgotten. As we traveled the ancient paths and stumbled over foundations that lay in ruin, I remember asking silently, "Lord, what is it You're doing? Why are we here?"

His presence settled heavily on me there in the old city of Jerusalem. "Look upon Zion, the city of our appointed feasts," the quiet voice answered (see Is. 33:20). I looked up from the rocks to the others in our tour group. No one else had heard the voice. Then I caught my daughter's glance, had she heard it too?

> *...Look to the rock from which you were hewn, and to the quarry from which you were dug. Look to Abraham your father...* (Isaiah 51:1-2).

"Yes, Lord," I answered under my breath. "But Abraham...?" I questioned, "I'm not Jewish." I was excited to be there, though this trip had never been planned or even discussed before the phone call.

> *By faith Abraham, when he was called, obeyed by going out to a place which he was to receive for an inheritance.... For he was looking for the city which has foundations, whose architect and builder is God* (Hebrews 11:8,10).

> *His foundation is in the holy mountains. The Lord loves the gates of Zion* (Psalm 87:1).

I looked up at the wall, then back down at the rocks. "Can God really speak through the rocks?" I wondered.

"Surely the stone will cry out from the wall..." (Hab. 2:11). That was the beginning, and it was with great joy that we returned to Jerusalem seven years later as watchmen during the Jewish *Feast of Tabernacles*, a seven day celebration. Seven members of our family went that time.

There were seven feasts that were celebrated in the Old Testament, and the *Feast of Tabernacles* was one of the three main feasts that every male Israelite was commanded to observe each year, under the law of Moses.

Seven days you shall celebrate a feast to the Lord your God in the place which the Lord chooses, because the Lord your God will bless you in all your produce and in all the work of your hands, so that you shall be altogether joyful (Deuteronomy 16:15).

So we went to Jerusalem. And we were altogether joyful, although we weren't quite sure why we were there.

"And [Abraham] went out, not knowing where he was going" (Heb. 11:8b). Rebekah also, when she was called, went into a strange land, to become the bride of a man she had never met.

Then they called Rebekah and said to her, "will you go with this man?" And she said, "I will go" (Genesis 24:58).

How about you? Will you go with us, to an unknown place? We have not passed this way before (see Josh. 3:4).

Set for yourselves roadmarks, place for yourself guideposts; direct your mind to the highway, the way by which you went. Return, O virgin Israel, return to these your cities. How long will you go here and there, O faithless daughter? For the Lord has created a new thing in the earth—A woman will encompass a man (Jeremiah 31:21-22).

Would you feel more comfortable in familiar surroundings, among friends? We are going soon, and we do have a road map. "...A highway will be there, a roadway...it will be for him who walks that way, and fools will not wander on it" (Is. 35:8). "And your ears will hear a word behind you, 'This is the way, walk in it'..." (Is. 30:21). "...I am the way, the truth, and the life; no one comes to the Father, but through Me" (Jn. 14:6).

This is the generation of those who seek Him..... Lift up your heads, O gates, and be lifted up, O ancient doors, that the King of glory may come in! (Psalm 24:6-7).

And I set watchmen over you, saying "Listen to the sound of the trumpet!" (Jeremiah 6:17a)

The trumpet has sounded!

Come, *Go Through the Gates*, to the mountain of the Lord. You're wondering: *Does God have a plan? If He does, what is it? Why does He allow sin and evil in the world? Does He really care about us—about "me"? Does He care what is happening here on the earth today?*

Chapter 1

The Garden Gate

When I consider Thy heavens, the work of Thy fingers, the moon and the stars, which Thou has ordained; what is man, that Thou dost take thought of him? (Psalm 8:3-4a)

There was no gate in the Garden of Eden. We think of a gate because of the Cherubim that was set at the east of the garden, guarding the way to the tree of life; however that happened after Adam and Eve fell into sin.

We wonder what really happened in the garden at that time: *Why does God allow sin and evil to exist in the world? Does God have a plan, or did Adam and Eve mess it up? Does He have things under control, or is He just winging it? Does He care about man and what happens to him here on earth?*

By weaving the stories and prophecies of the Old Testament within the teachings of Jesus and the apostles (including the New Testament Book of Revelation), the fabric of God's perfect plan begins to emerge.

We know that God created all things, but we shall primarily concern ourselves with the creation of Man on the sixth day.

And God saw all that He had made, and behold, it was very good... (Genesis 1:31).

He had just finished creating man and since He Himself made him, God certainly knew that man was capable of falling into sin. There was no mistake. Man was no accident or embarrassment to God. He was created in God's own image, and the intention was that he should rule over every living thing that moves on the earth (see Gen. 1:26). He was given dominion over the earth. God was pleased with His creation and He had a definite long-range plan from the beginning. He isn't just improvising as we go along.

Imagine stretching out the heavens!

Only God could possibly know how to separate light from darkness. We wouldn't even be able to comprehend light if we had never experienced it. We still can't explain it.

It was important for light to be separated from darkness; they are two different forces. Jesus said, "I am the light of the world" (Jn. 8:12). The apostle Paul asks, "...What fellowship has light with darkness?" (2 Cor. 6:14) In other words, they don't belong together. We always connect the thought of satan with darkness. So in the beginning God separated the light from the darkness—first in the natural, then in the spiritual (see 1 Cor. 15:46).

After that He proceeded with the rest of creation. Out of the chaotic nothingness, He spoke things into being, and He set the tides on an exact table. The tides come in and go out. The sun rises and sets. Everything has run in perfect order down through the centuries. The light shines and the plants grow. In the fall, the trees drop their leaves and the birds go south. You can count on it.

But what about Man?

"What is Man that Thou rememberest him?" (Heb. 2:6) Man is God's best—"fearfully and wonderfully made" (Ps. 139:14).

We sometimes feel that mankind is getting out of control, but in God His wisdom would never permit this.

He could have made man with instincts like the birds and animals but He had a much better idea. He decided to give man a free will. He already had angels to do His bidding. He deliberately made man to be different. Man was designed at a higher level of creation, and God was pleased. Now man could make a choice whether to look to God or go his own way. This was immensely interesting to God. A free will would be of no value if there weren't opposing forces. God wants man to prevail and overcome the darkness.

Adam was allowed to name all the animals. Then God saw that none of them would be suitable as a companion for Adam, so He made woman to be his wife that they might become one flesh. The woman was taken from the body of the first Adam.

We have no way of knowing how long Adam and Eve lived in this idyllic setting in the Garden of Eden where in their innocence they had no worries or frustrations. If they were hungry they ate fruit from the trees and the green plant (see Gen. 9:3).

They had no anxiety regarding what was right or wrong and no consciousness of time, sickness or death. These are our daily concerns. They had direct communion with their maker; God walked in the garden and talked with them. He wasn't way off somewhere past the stars and clouds, but He was there with them on earth.

The animals must have been friendly. The serpent spoke to Eve, and the first thing he said was a lie. Eve knew God's instructions that they could eat from any tree in the garden except the tree of the knowledge of good and evil, but we read that the serpent was more crafty (cunning) than any other beast of the field that God had made. He cleverly appealed to Eve's intelligence, causing her to question God's word:

...Indeed, has God said "You shall not eat from any tree of the garden"? ...You surely shall not die! (Genesis 3:1,4)

The friendly serpent (who probably was walking upright at the time, since he was forced to crawl on his belly in the dust after the curse) must have pulled himself up to full stature, and with a broad smile assured the woman, "Oh no, it's not true. You won't die, trust me."

Thus the classic lie of satan was spoken for the first time on earth, but it was certainly not the last time. The lie remains pretty much the same. It usually goes something like this: "Surely you don't believe that just because it's in the Bible? After all, God created you with great intelligence and a free will. He surely expects you to use what you have in making decisions, and besides, He's such a loving God. He would never let anyone go to Hell."

Isn't it interesting that the tempter didn't say anything about the fruit being delicious? They had plenty to eat, and the appetite was not the area in which he planned to tempt Eve. It appears that pride, covetousness, and lust for power were the things calculated as the appropriate stimulus for tempting her, because he told her she could be like God if she ate the fruit.

Entertaining that thought briefly, Adam and Eve fell into sin and then the curse was activated,

By the sweat of your face you shall eat bread, till you return to the ground, because from it you were taken; for you are dust, and to dust you shall return (Genesis 3:19).

There went their eternal life! Thorns and thistles would be their future.

The fall was great. Much was at stake, and much was lost in that seemingly insignificant act of rebellion.

Adam and Eve gave it all away to satan, the deceiver. The dominion was gone. Adam really "blew it" during his probation period, and he was driven from the garden to the place where death would await him. He was no longer in God's presence, no longer a ruler, and eternal life was snatched from him.

The cherubim were there acting as a gate to make sure no one could come near the tree of life. After that if Adam wanted to eat, he would have to contend with rocks, clods, weeds, and briars as he cultivated the ground in the heat of the day with sweat forming on his brow.

The moment they sinned, they experienced guilt, fear, and frustration—guilt over what they had done, fear that God would know they did it, and frustration over what to do about it.

They quickly made a covering of fig leaves for their bodies, and when God came walking in the garden in the cool of the day, they foolishly tried to hide from the Lord God, whose company they had enjoyed before sin entered their lives.

Suddenly they were naked! They had lost their covering of God's presence.

They were now in the realm of the flesh, and it would be a long journey back to that place in God's presence.

What does it mean when it says that Adam was created in God's image? God is Spirit. Does it mean Adam was a spirit?

We know he was a man, made from the dust of the earth, but something must have changed about his body because he suddenly noticed he was naked. And God clothed him with skin (see Gen. 3:21). I believe Adam and Eve were clothed in God's glory and the light of His presence before they sinned. I believe they were light bearers meant to reflect God's light and glory (His character and nature) here on earth.

All of that came to an end with the serpent's suggestions that they could be like God. It would seem that before that thought of rebellion, they were like little children. In their innocence, they would have asked the Father what to do; they would have looked to Him for guidance in their decisions. Immediately after their act of disobedience, they started making their own decisions, putting fig leaves together for loin coverings, hiding from God, and lying.

Little children are darling. We like having them look up to us, but sooner or later, every child has to grow up and start making his own decisions, even though he may make some poor judgments at first. We don't want him to be near us simply because he has no choice, but because he has chosen it. When first learning to walk, we smile indulgently at a child as he pulls the vase from the coffee table, but Adam's act—that was something else. He really did a whopper!

One thing that stands out, like a flag that cannot be ignored: Before the fall Adam and Eve were "God" centered; and after the fall, they were "self" centered.

They were originally created complete—body, soul, and spirit. The soul part of us is made of the mind, personality, will, and emotions. Adam and Eve still had their bodies and souls; however, they died spiritually. They lost their original estate—the place of God's presence, the position of dominion, and their eternal life.

At that time there was only one kind of man on the earth (Adam), so with the fall, all of mankind became destined for death until Jesus came. He was a victorious, overcoming man who became a life-giving spirit.

..."The first man, Adam, became a living soul." The last Adam [Jesus] became a life-giving spirit (1 Corinthians 15:45).

When He came with the new covenant, a way was made for us, so rather than being destined for death, all who are in Christ are destined for resurrection.

...Christ in you, the hope of glory (Colossians 1:27).

Therefore, just as through one man [Adam] sin entered into the world...who is a type of Him who was to come (Romans 5:12,14b).

We know, of course, that the one who was to come was Jesus Christ.

So then as through one transgression there resulted condemnation to all men, even so through one act of righteousness there resulted justification of life to all men (Romans 5:18).

We've heard all these Scriptures before, but what do they mean to us?

They mean everything to us; we're talking about God's plan for man's restoration. God has destined us for great things. Did you ever see a kid who you never thought could amount to anything; yet miraculously, he turned out fine? Often this has to do with the father.

The fact that Adam transgressed the covenant didn't throw God's plan out of kilter. (Did you give up on your son because he broke a vase while he was learning to walk?) God is all wise and He knew from the beginning what might happen, so He merely set the next phase of His plan in motion.

If Jesus is the last Adam, what about us?

In the New Testament, the apostle Paul talks a lot about the "new man" who is a new creation, with old things having passed away (see 2 Cor. 5:17), a man who is being conformed to the image of Christ.

You guessed it. Jesus is our pattern. We'll be talking more about this important truth.

We live at a time when certain epochs pertaining to this plan of God's will culminate—things that the prophets wrote about and that the angels would like to see happen.

After the fall, Eve conceived and gave birth to Cain, proudly announcing, "I have gotten a manchild with the help of the Lord" (Gen. 4:1b).

Ostensibly, Eve understood perfectly what "was to have been" in the original scheme of things. She knew that God's plan was for the manchild to be reproduced through the woman, but her wisdom was already deteriorating; she didn't comprehend the fact that their sin effected a change in that plan. Eve's first manchild killed his brother Abel in a jealous rage because the Lord liked Abel's sacrifice and rejected his own.

Sin was already working out its course.

Eve conceived again and gave birth to Seth, and she said, "God has appointed me another offspring in place of [substitute for] Abel..." (Gen. 4:25b).

In examining God's plan we notice that He is selective. He accepted Abel's blood sacrifice but rejected Cain's offer of the fruit of the ground. We read in First John 3:12 that the works of Cain were evil and his brother's were righteous. Cain added to his guilt by the denial of his act, his lack of repentance, and his attitude of rebellion. He ran away to the land of Nod where he built a city, the first of many of man's undertakings apart from God.

This story seems to be a prefigure or shadow of the holy nation of Israel failing to bring forth fruit, and a substitute being provided as salvation came to the gentiles. Spiritually, Seth prefigures Christ; faith came through Seth.

We will now leave the garden scene where history was first framed. We will leave Adam and Eve, the serpent, the cherubim, and the manchild at the east of the garden where they were driven. Later in this book we will again come upon a similar combination (in the twelfth chapter of Revelation)—the woman, the dragon, the manchild, and the angel Michael.

Chapter 2

The Floodgates of the Sky

*...the fountains of the great deep burst open, and the **floodgates of the sky** were opened. And the rain fell upon the earth for forty days and forty nights* (Genesis 7:11-12).

At one time God was actually sorry He had made man, since the wickedness was so great on the earth. Man's thoughts were continually on evil. It grieved God, and He decided to blot man out from the face of the earth, along with all the animals, birds, and creeping things. But Noah found favor in God's eyes. He alone was found to be righteous before God. Think of it! One righteous man in a perverse world filled with violence—He wouldn't have been popular.

God was about to bring destruction upon the earth, so He told Noah to build an ark for himself, his wife, his three sons, and their wives—eight people. (In biblical symbolism, the number eight stands for new beginnings.)

He gave Noah all the details of how the ark was to be built. It was to be made of certain woods, have certain measurements, etc. It was to have three decks—a lower, a second, and a third deck. He was to take pairs of all the animals, birds, and creeping things with him into the ark, as well as food for his family and the animals.

This man, who was unique in his righteousness, was warned one hundred and twenty years before the flood.

While engaged in this colossal undertaking, he was also diligently preaching righteousness to a world that did not want to hear his message or repent.

Noah heard God's voice and obeyed.

He was prepared. Building an ark wasn't something you could put off until the last minute, but he was able to take his entire family with him. Seven days before the flood, God told Noah to get in the ark, and He closed the door behind them.

Sure enough, seven days later the fountains of the great deep burst open, the *floodgates of the sky* were opened, and the rain fell for forty days and forty nights.

Then the flood came upon the earth for forty days; and the water increased and lifted up the ark, so that it rose above the earth (Genesis 7:17).

The story of Noah and the ark has always been a favorite of children because of all the animals. As a child, it seemed like a party to me. I could just picture that big boat bobbing along up above the earth, as the wicked and perverse things were swept away below.

When I grew older I could imagine the problems and unpleasantness involved with the confinement; however they were safe, and God remembered Noah and the animals (see Gen. 8:10).

The water prevailed upon the earth for one hundred and fifty days. And on the seventeenth day of the seventh month, the ark "rested" on the mountains of Ararat (a high and lofty place).

This date is rather interesting, for it coincides with the date of the *Feast of Tabernacles,* which God instructed Moses to institute and observe in Israel. It was to be celebrated for seven days each year, starting with the fifteenth day of the seventh month (Lev. 23:39).

This is mentioned here (and will be mentioned again later), because it appears that these three important feasts of the Old Testament represent the three steps toward the maturity of the believer. Two of the three feasts have already been fulfilled through Christ in the New Testament—the *Feast of Passover,* which pointed to the blood of Jesus; and the *Feast of Pentecost,* which was fulfilled in the upper room through the coming of the Holy Spirit at the beginning of the Age of Grace (or Church Age).

The Bible is a book of numerical perfection, a book coming from God who is infinite to man in the natural realm. It cannot be understood without the help of the Holy Spirit. To the natural man it is foolishness (see 1 Cor. 2:14). In order to properly understand it, one must be born of the Spirit (Jn. 3:6) and filled with the Spirit (Eph. 5:18-19). Otherwise it remains a closed book, just words without meaning. However, the numbers, symbols, and rhythms become an exciting and challenging puzzle for the seeker who digs deeper into the Bible. Those who follow the lamb wherever He goes (see Rev. 14:4) find Jesus throughout the pages of Scripture, and they can't get enough of Him and His glory.

Who can fathom God's giant computer, one that stores information on every person who ever lived—with his or her name written in a book waiting to be checked off? Who can understand someone that can inspire a book with stories about actual people and happenings thousands of years ago, which are being re-enacted once more through real people in our day? Our minds can't take it all in, but God is the creator of all things. He possesses all wisdom!

Exactly one year after the floodgates were opened, the earth was dry. Noah built an altar and offered burnt offerings that pleased God, for then He said to Himself, "I will never again curse the ground on account of man" (see Gen. 8:21).

So God established a covenant with Noah and his sons, and He put the rainbow in the sky as a sign of the covenant. (No wonder children love this story.)

It took dynamic faith for Noah to believe all that time, when he was building the ark and waiting for the flood. After all, they had never before had rain, so how could he imagine a flood? The mists had always watered the earth until that time. Never before had they seen torrential rain.

The Floodgates of the Sky

After the flood, the people who were in the ark inherited the earth, along with God's blessings. It appears that meat was added to their diet at that time, whereas the green plant and fruit had been sufficient before (Gen. 9:3).

Chapter 3

Gate of God

...Come, let us make bricks. ...Let us build for ourselves a city... (Genesis 11:4).

Not too long after the flood, there was an unusual project begun in the plains of Shinar, near the mountains of Ararat. At that time everyone spoke the same language even though the nations had been separated after the flood. Men had become fascinated with the idea of building. Cain, for example, departed from God's company after he killed Abel and ran away to the land of Nod where he built a city.

This group had gotten together and decided to build a city with a tower that would reach into heaven. They decided they would use bricks for their work.

Like little boys building a fort in the vacant lot, they wanted to make a name for themselves that would show they were all of one mind and strength, unified in fellowship, so they wouldn't get separated. (Fraternal groups and congregations have been doing the same thing ever since.)

There is a certain feeling of pride and security in belonging to a group or organization. Those on the plains of Shinar said to one another,

> ...*Come, let us build for ourselves a city, and a tower whose top will reach into heaven, and let us make for ourselves a name; lest we be scattered abroad over the face of the whole earth* (Genesis 11:4).

They probably felt they could get more accomplished and would have more power and influence if they banded together to do this monumental thing. Their fame would spread, and their name would be known far and wide.

God was quite concerned about this humanistic endeavor that was based in rebellion against God. The Lord said,

> ...*Behold, they are one people, and they all have the same language, and this is what they began to do, and now nothing which they purpose to do will be impossible for them* (Genesis 11:6).

He put an end to it then and there. God confused their language and scattered them over the face of the earth.

They named the place *Babel*, which means confusion. In the original application of the name it meant *Gate of God*.

They didn't care about worshipping Noah's God. They wanted to get to Heaven through their own efforts and intellect. They probably planned to use the tower for their astrology by getting closer to the stars. The people of Babel thought the tower was a great idea. Everyone looks up to a tower, and towers are highly visible.

These people were the "do-ers" of their day, ahead of others and definitely into the "in" thing at that time, which was building. It is thought that Nimrod, grandson of Ham, was the leader of this enterprise. This man was fired with ambition and "became a mighty one on earth" (Gen. 10:8). He was a hunter and a builder—a builder apart from God it would appear.

It is noteworthy that they learned to make bricks, using tar for mortar. They used bricks in place of stone. Brick structures will last hundreds of years, but stone buildings and walls last thousands. Bricks are manmade and all of the same size and shape, so you can build faster. They can be formed quickly and conform easily to other bricks.

Stone may be more interesting and beautiful to look at, but it takes more time and effort for stones to be fitted together, since each stone is unique, formed from the pressures of the elements and by God. In the New Testament, Peter says that we are stones being fitted together.

You also, as living stones, are being built up as a spiritual house for a holy priesthood... (1 Peter 2:5).

Satan always has his counterfeits, so I imagine he had something to do with that fiasco with the bricks—where God had to step in and stop it.

Our Master Builder has a long attention span. His main purpose in calling Israel as a nation unto Himself, beginning with Abraham, was to form them into a holy priesthood. Then in the New Testament, fifteen hundred years later, Peter explains to the believers that they are stones being built into a spiritual house for a holy priesthood. Also the psalmist speaks of the stone that the builders rejected that has become the chief cornerstone (see Ps. 118:22; Mt. 21:42).

I think it would be safe to say that God didn't like the building that the people of Babel were doing. After He took action work on the city stopped.

The Tower of Babel seems to be a symbol or foreshadow of the many future systems of man.

Chapter 4

Gate of Sodom

*Now the two angels came to Sodom in the evening as Lot was sitting in the **gate of Sodom**...* (Genesis 19:1).

The Creator of the universe is not easily distracted by a few troubling incidents like the Tower of Babel. A couple of millenia had passed since Adam and Eve had left the garden, and God's plan was still going forward.

Time is no obstacle to the one God who dwells in eternity. Who can fathom it?

What is man that God is mindful of him? (Ps. 8:4; Heb. 2:6)

There was a man named Abram who was just the kind of man God was looking for. God said to Abram,

...Go forth from your country and from your relatives, and from your father's house, to the land which I will

show you; and I will make you a great nation... (Genesis 12:1-2).

Abram "heard" Him when He spoke. In reviewing these Old Testament stories, we are already finding examples of two types of men, consequent to the fall. Through all the noise and din of a perverse and wicked world, Noah "heard" God when He spoke. Now we come across Abram, who lived more or less as a contemporary of Nimrod the rebel builder. And we read that Abram heard God when He spoke while others didn't.

Abram descended from Shem, and Nimrod from Ham. Noah had cursed Ham's son Canaan after he and his father uncovered Noah's nakedness.

When Abram heard, he quickly obeyed. He took his barren wife Sarai and his nephew Lot along with him.

This was a different picture from that of the Tower of Babel where man was trying to build his way up to Heaven in his own strength, ignoring God. This was God reaching down to man, wanting to bless him, and through this man God wanted to bless the world.

Abram, whose name was later changed to Abraham, was a man who went looking for a city. He didn't know where it was, but he knew that its builder and maker was God (Heb. 11:10). He had a vision.

He didn't seem interested in the cities being built by man.

What made him go? The apostle Paul said,

By faith Abraham, when he was called, obeyed by going out to a place which he was to receive for an inheritance;

and he went out, not knowing where he was going (Hebrews 11:8).

Stephen, speaking before the council in Jerusalem, said,

...The God of glory appeared to our father Abraham when he was in Mesopotamia... (Acts 7:2).

That explains to me his willingness to pull up stakes and go. If the God of glory appears, He definitely has your attention. Abram surely must have had a vision of a glorious city, and everything else paled in comparison.

In the war of the kings, when Abram came back from the battle where he defeated Chedorlaomer and the kings, Abram gave a tenth of all the spoils to Melchizedek, king of Salem (peace).

He refused the offer of the king of Sodom, however, and told him, "I will not take a thread or a sandal thong, or anything that is yours, lest you should say 'I have made Abram rich' " (see Gen. 14:23).

He knew the source of his riches, and Abram was destined to be rich no matter what. The hand of God was on him; so he went. He took his wife Sarai and his nephew Lot (even though Lot wasn't called by God). Abram and his wife were old, past the age of childbearing, and Sarai had always been barren. Yet God promised them a son. So after some time had gone by, Sarai decided to get things going and help God out by offering her maid to Abram (according to the custom at that time). After all, ten years had gone by, and at their age...?

So Hagar, Sarai's Egyptian maid, slept with Abram and conceived a child. Then when she realized she was going to have Abram's child, she suddenly despised her mistress Sarai.

This troubled Sarai, so she complained to her husband. He told her that since Hagar was her slave, she could do whatever she wished with her.

Sarai was harsh with Hagar, so she ran away. Hagar was alone and pregnant out in the wilderness when the Lord came to her and told her to go back and submit to her mistress' authority. From this example, I think she represents God's people and their need to submit to the authority of the Holy Spirit. The angel told Hagar that God had given heed to her affliction. She would have a son, and his name would be Ishmael,

And he will be a wild donkey of a man, his hand will be against everyone, and everyone's hand will be against him; and he will live to the east of all his brothers (Genesis 16:12).

Ishmael is the father of the Arab nations.

Thirteen years later the Lord appeared to Abram. God gave him the covenant of circumcision, changing Abram's name to Abraham, and his wife's name from Sarai to Sarah. Once again God promised them a son.

At that point Abraham probably thought He was referring to Ishmael, but God assured him that it would not be Ishmael, the child of the bondwoman, but that Sarah would indeed bear him a son.

But My covenant I will establish with Isaac, whom Sarah will bear to you at this season next year (Genesis 17:21).

By then so many years had gone by that Abraham may have had moments when he thought, "Lord, Sarah is getting old. Don't let her die before this child is born." But God "remembered" Sarah and the promise, and Isaac was born.

When Isaac was growing to maturity, God asked Abraham to sacrifice him, and we all know the touching story of Abraham's obedience when he was tested (see Gen. 22:1-18).

On the third day, Abraham took Isaac to the mountain and prepared him as a sacrifice, then at the last moment God told him not to touch his son. Instead a ram was caught in the nearby thicket, and it was provided as a substitute offering (Gen. 22:13).

This plainly foreshadows the blood atonement of Jesus, as He became a substitute (the Lamb that was slain) for our sins. He took them all upon Himself (see Jn. 1:29). Seth was a substitute for Abel. Isaac is also a type of Christ. He represents Christ and the covenant people—he was the seed of Abraham through which the covenant was established.

At that time the Lord swore to Abraham that because he had not withheld his own son, his seed would "possess the gate of their enemies" (see Gen. 22:17).

Two thousand years later, Jesus said, "...I will build My church; and the gates of Hades shall not overpower it" (Mt. 16:18). This hasn't really been fulfilled, but we know that if we are in Christ, we are Abraham's seed. And God promised Abraham that his seed would possess the gate of the enemy!

We can be sure that Jesus will build His Church. (We can't build it because we *are* His Church, or called-out people.) Satan will not be able to prevail against it.

Even the language in this story points forward toward Jesus, God's own Son whom He did not withhold in planning our redemption.

The three messengers (angels), who came to tell Abraham about the approaching birth of Isaac in the year before he was born, were on their way to check out the city of Sodom. The sin in that city was exceedingly grave.

As they were leaving after finishing a meal with Abraham, the three messengers looked down toward Sodom. The Lord said, "Shall I hide from Abraham what I am about to do?" (Gen. 18:17) Abraham was God's friend, and God knew Abraham's nephew Lot was in that perverse city. Compare this to what the prophet Amos wrote much later,

Surely the Lord God does nothing unless He reveals His secret counsel to His servants the prophets (Amos 3:7).

In other words, God wants to communicate with His people.

He was about to destroy the wicked city of Sodom! The conversation that followed showed there weren't even ten righteous people in the whole city.

The two angels who went on to Sodom in the evening found Lot sitting in the *gate of Sodom*. The gate was where all business, bargaining, news, and gossip exchanges took place, so Lot was definitely part of the city life.

He never intended to become involved there. He was really an alien, but maybe he stayed too long and became more or less accustomed to their ways.

He showed reverence when the angels appeared, and he urged them to partake of his hospitality. He did everything he could to protect them from the men of Sodom who had come to rape them, but Lot was strongly oppressed by the Sodomites. They were furious with him for protecting the visitors and said,

..."*This one came in as an alien, and already he is acting like a judge...*" (Genesis 19:9).

This prophetic statement unknowingly made by the Sodomites stretches forward, clear into the New Testament times. It points to the fact that God's chosen ones, His holy priesthood, though aliens in this world will one day judge the world and even the angels (see 1 Cor. 6:2).

These men of Sodom were acting wickedly, insisting on having their own way. Finally the angels had to blind the men and pull Lot inside the house.

At the dawning of the day, the angels said to Lot,

Up, take your wife and your two daughters, who are here, lest you be swept away in the punishment of the city (Genesis 19:15b).

When they hesitated, the angels literally took their hands and led them to where they would be safe outside the city. They were told, "Escape for your lives, Don't look back. Escape to the mountains" (see Gen. 19:17).

Lot's wife didn't make it. She had to have one last look, and she became a pillar of salt. Lot barely got out with his life, and that was only because he was Abraham's nephew.

When God destroyed the cities of the valley...God remembered Abraham, and sent Lot out... (Genesis 19:29).

Lot had instructions concerning his escape, just as Noah had instructions ahead of time, but Lot didn't follow them perfectly. He wanted to talk, argue, and do it his way. He was glad to be safe, but he must have had a fondness for the city life. Actually, he had a fear of going to the mountain, for he thought he might die. So he asked God if he couldn't just stay there in the little town nearby because it was "just a small town." The mountain was something unknown and unfamiliar to him. He felt he would be able to find fellowship there in the little city.

Lot eventually did go to the mountains, but he wasn't in God's timing and direction. He was so frightened when he saw the destruction of Sodom that he went up on the mountain and hid in a cave where he was debased in an orgy with his daughters. They were intent upon securing their own futures and making their own decisions when they planned the incestuous scheme. The two sons born out of that debauchery were named Moab and Ammon (Gen. 19:30).

It is interesting to follow them and their descendents throughout the Bible; they were always standing against Israel. They were cruel, wealthy, idolatrous, and prideful. Captivity, desolation, and destruction was prophesied for them by Isaiah, Jeremiah, and Amos.

Meanwhile Abraham was walking on the high ground where he had chosen to dwell, and he was left undisturbed by the destruction of Sodom.

We know that, as a type, Egypt represents the world or the world systems. So in this story, I see Sarai as representing God's people, Israel. She didn't trust God to do this momentous thing, so she wanted to help God (work for God) by using Hagar, the slave maid. Hagar was Egyptian (worldly), so Sarai ended up with Ishmael, which was not part of God's plan. Sarai (who later became Sarah) had been barren until Isaac (a representative of Jesus) was born.

The apostle Paul explained in Galatians 4:25-30 how these two women represent two different covenants. Hagar, the bondwoman or slave, allegorically represents Sinai (the Law). She is like the Jerusalem of Paul's day consumed by the Law and personal works, and she was in slavery with her children (also born of the flesh, part of the worldly way).

Paul then explained that the brethren he was talking to—those in the early Church reaching up to us today—are part of the Jerusalem above. We are free, not in slavery, and "the Jerusalem above...is the mother of us all" (see Gal. 4:26). Under Moses, the tabernacle in the wilderness was made according to the pattern he saw in heaven (the free Jerusalem). The tabernacle was a portable shrine that went everywhere with the Israelites. This was a foreshadow of the "new thing" that would replace the Law after Jesus came with the ultimate sacrifice, including the later sending of the Holy Spirit, the "treasure in earthen vessels" of Second Corinthians 4:7. This way God could meet with us wherever we go. *We are the temple under the New Covenant, and the temple is portable* (see Rev. 3:12; 21:2). This is the New Jerusalem that will come down from Heaven as a bride. In that day the tabernacle of God will be "among men"; God Himself shall be among them (Rev. 21:2).

This is the city Abraham saw in his vision, the city he was looking for. Those who "overcome" shall inherit these things:

...and I will be his God and he shall be My son (Revelation 21:7).

Chapter 5

Gate of Heaven

Hagar and Ishmael were eventually separated from Abraham's household. When Isaac was weaned, Abraham gave a feast and Sarai saw Ishmael mocking. Her husband heard about it, and at God's urging he sent the bond-slave and her son away.

This rivalry persists even today in the antagonisms between Arabs and Jews (in the natural realm.)

This book is primarily concerned with the spiritual aspect of this on-going parallel—the story of the "land of Israel" and the corresponding story of the Church through the centuries. It has been well said that if you want to know how the Church is doing, you should take a look at the state of Israel.

It was a miracle when the nation of Israel was born in the spring of 1948 after the land had laid for centuries as a wasted wilderness. Bible scholars before the turn of the century were well aware of the Scriptures concerning the re-gathering of the Jews. They had sometimes tried to stretch their faith to accommodate such a scenario, but one look at pitiful, parched Palestine made it seem highly unlikely that the prophecies would ever come to pass.

The Zionist movement was begun at the turn of the century. At about the same time there was a great worldwide outpouring of the Holy Ghost...the first, really, since Pentecost. The Holy Spirit was involved in the early Protestant movement but not worldwide.

The passing of another forty years brought the fresh revival of 1948 along with the new state of Israel, the rights of which Ishmael solidly refuses to acknowledge to this day.

Beginning in about 1967, another wave of the Holy Spirit swept over the continents. It spread like a brushfire in every direction. This also matched the time of the startling news that the Jews had regained control of the old city of Jerusalem after all those centuries. With that news, Bible scholars around the world found a renewed interest in the prophecies concerning the last days.

There was great joy in the camps of both the natural state of Israel and the spiritual Israel, the true Church. God's plan is moving right along, and that plan involves both the Church and the Jews. There will be one Kingdom.

What excitement we felt when we returned to Jerusalem after seven years. We found the Jewish quarter of the old city beautifully decked out with flowers, park benches, and smart shops—a consequence of the success of the restoration project begun earlier. It was exhilarating to know that during the same period truth was being restored to the Church and beauty to the streets of Jerusalem. (This is an illustration of the principle of first in the natural then in the spiritual [see 1 Cor. 15:46]).

With the casting away of Ishmael and Hagar, God began developing His carefully chosen line. As much as Abraham loved Ishmael, his first child, who was born in his old age, it would not be through Ishmael that the covenant would be established, but through Isaac, born of Sarah, the free woman.

Isaac grew to maturity, and as a part of this handpicked line a bride had to be chosen for Isaac. They went to Abraham's country and brought back Rebekah. Like Abraham, she was willing to journey into a strange land to become the bride of a man she had never seen. Rebekah conceived, and the twins struggled together within her. When she asked the Lord about it He said,

> ...*Two nations are in your womb; and two peoples shall be separated from your body; and one people shall be stronger than the other, and the older shall serve the younger* (Genesis 25:23).

Thus the story of Jacob and Esau begins.

Esau loved the excitement of the field and was a hunter. Jacob remained in his father's house. Esau came in famished from the hunt one day and traded his birthright for a bowl of stew that he smelled cooking. Not only did Jacob gain the birthright but his father's blessing as well, so Esau bore a grudge.

God had found the right man in Abraham. Next came Isaac, the child of promise in the chosen line. Then the plan really got going with Jacob, the God-favored son of Isaac.

One night Jacob had a dream. In the dream a ladder was set on earth, its top reaching to Heaven. (Wouldn't the men of Babel have loved that?) The angels of God were ascending and descending on this ladder, and the Lord stood above it and said,

> ...*I am the Lord, the God of your father Abraham and the God of Isaac; the land on which you lie, I will give it to you and your descendants* (Genesis 28:13).

He repeated to Jacob everything He had said previously to Abraham and Isaac. When Jacob awoke from his sleep, he said, "Surely the Lord is in this place.... This is none other than the house of God, and this is the Gate of Heaven (Gen. 28:15,17b). A stairway between earth and heaven—what a wondrous vision! Jacob made a pillar, poured oil on it, and made a vow to God. He called it "God's house." (This is surprising to discover; we will see later in the book just exactly what God's house is.)

Jacob knew God was re-affirming the covenant promise, but he must have been amazed at the stairway to heaven. A similar thing happened in the New Testament. Nathaniel was surprised when Jesus knew he had been in the fig tree that was blocks away, but Jesus told him,

> *...I say to you, you shall see the heavens opened, and the angels of God ascending and descending on the Son of Man* (John 1:51).

In other words, it may have seemed unbelievable to Nathaniel because he had been too far away for anyone to have been able to naturally see him, but Jesus was trying to tell him, "Just wait until you see what happens when I return." Heaven was opened to the apostle John too, on the Isle of Patmos.

Now with Jacob and Esau, we once again have two distinct types of men. Jacob was at the house seeing to family needs while Esau was out "doing his thing" wherever the excitement was. Then Esau held a grudge against Jacob because of giving up the birthright and losing the blessing to him. They were back at it again; they had struggled against each other even in the womb.

When interpreting the spiritual significance of the story of Abraham, Paul explained to the Galatians that the two women represent two covenants. The son of the bondwoman was born "according to the flesh," while the son of the free woman, Sarah, was born "according to the promise" (Gal. 4:23). The bondwoman and her son had to be cast out because the bondwoman's son could not be an heir with the son of the free woman. (Before you start getting bored with all this, read on; it has to do with you and me.)

Paul told the New Testament believers that they, like Isaac, were children of the promise and shouldn't be under the Law as some had tried to teach them. He ended by saying,

> *But as at that time he who was born according to the flesh persecuted him who was born according to the Spirit, so it is now also* (Galatians 4:29).

Esau lost his inheritance, and in the providence of God, he was made subservient to Jacob. (Esau represents the flesh.) We don't hear much about Esau's sons, but we hear plenty about the sons of Israel (Jacob's sons). They became the twelve tribes of Israel.

Jacob's name was changed to Israel after he wrestled with the angel all through the night. He had to admit to the angel, to the Lord, that his name was *Jacob*, which means supplanter, coercer, finagler, manipulator, etc.

Hebrew names all have meanings. For example, Judah means "praise"; Gad means "troop"; and Asher means "Happy." It's interesting to take the meaning of each of the names of the twelve sons of Israel and arrange them in sequence—with a result something like this:

> A happy troop of sons, hearing from God, joined by His Spirit, praising Him even in uncertainty increase in faith while wrestling with the flesh. Sons of the right hand, born at the end of the age, they will judge.

This would seem to be a prophetic projection reaching far into the future, picturing the Melchizedek priesthood of our Lord Jesus Christ. Priests and kings who will reign with Him on earth for a thousand years: this is God's plan for Abraham's seed beginning with Isaac. The name Melchizedek means "righteousness."

Isaiah prophesied of the righteous reign of a branch springing from the root of Jesse (David's father). It would be a branch that would bear much fruit, one "on whom the Spirit of the Lord would rest" (Is. 11:1-2). He will stand as a signal for the peoples on "that day" when "...the Lord will again recover the second time with His hand, the remnant of His people...." (See Isaiah 11:1-11.)

Of the twelve sons of Israel, only Joseph and Benjamin were born of Jacob's beloved wife Rachel; she died when Benjamin was born. Benjamin was born after Jacob wrestled all through the night with the angel and his name was changed to Israel.

It's good to try and remember all these details as we get toward the end of the book and begin to figure out what some of these characters and figures are foreshadowing.

Continuing down the line of God's calling, we come to the bountiful story of Joseph, the favorite son of Jacob, who was given the brightly-colored, "priestly" coat by his father. This caused Joseph to be hated by his jealous older brothers. His dream about all his brothers' sheaves of wheat bowing down to his sheaf didn't help much either.

As if that weren't enough, this sensitive godly dreamer had another dream about the sun and moon and eleven stars bowing down to him. (Now get this, he had eleven brothers.) At this point, is it any wonder his brothers plotted to kill him? Sometimes it's best for a person to keep his dreams to himself.

At Judah's suggestions they ended up selling him to an Ishmaelite caravan headed for Egypt. They got twenty shekels of silver for their effort to do away with him. They hated having him around. True Jews are from the tribe of Judah.

So Joseph was taken to Egypt and sold as a slave, but just like his father Jacob, God prospered him in spite of any harmful plots against him (despite Laban's trickery, God came up with speckled and spotted cows to meet Jacob's need [see Gen. 30:39]).

Joseph went to Egypt as a slave, humbled and shamed, after he had once felt like a prince at home as his father's favorite. However, it wasn't long until he was Potipher's personal servant. He was then made overseer of the entire house and all Potipher owned. Then the Lord blessed the Egyptian's house because of Joseph's presence, so Potipher left Joseph in charge of everything.

Not only is this a good story, but it is clear that Joseph is a type of Jesus. Consider this as you review the story of Joseph.

Potipher's wife tried to seduce Joseph. She caused his imprisonment when he rejected her advances, but God was with him and gave him favor with the chief jailer. Soon he was in charge of all the prisoners who were bound. Whatever they needed, he could provide it for them.

By interpreting Pharaoh's dream and predicting the seven years of famine after seven years of plenty, the Egyptians were able to store all the grain needed. So

Joseph was put in charge of all the grain storage and was made a ruler in Egypt. (How I love this story.) Believe it or not, this story has to do with us!

"Behold, days are coming," declares the Lord God, "When I will send a famine on the land, not a famine for bread or a thirst for water, but rather for hearing the words of the Lord" (Amos 8:11).

Amos was one of several great prophetic figures who lived in an Old Testament period that was much like ours today. The people were experiencing prosperity, but there was also wickedness and corruption as never before. It seems that Amos was not only warning them but us as well; he was speaking against their spiritual decay and materialism. He confirmed God's disgust at their pretense of worship at their festivals and solemn assemblies; "the noise of their songs" (see Amos 5:21-23). He was talking to those who were at ease in Zion during Israel's last days of glory. He warned of judgment; the Lord would be heard in judgment from Zion. But at the same time, he conveyed promise of restoration for Israel when God would raise up the fallen booth of David.

Back in Joseph's time when the famine came and the people cried out for bread, Pharaoh would say, "Go to Joseph. He can take care of all your needs." Joseph was really their salvation at that time of great need (just as Jesus said, "I am the Bread of Life" [Jn. 6:48]).

When Jacob sent the brothers to get food in Egypt, Joseph recognized his brothers, but they didn't seem to know him. He knew their names. There is no question that Joseph prefigured Jesus: "I am the good shepherd; and I know My own..." (Jn. 10:14); "he calls his own sheep by name" (Jn. 10:3).

The first time Joseph's brothers went to Egypt to get grain, Joseph questioned them about their father. He instructed them to be sure to bring their youngest brother when they came back for more grain. The famine was severe, even in Canaan, so when they were ready to go back, they told their father what the keeper of the grain had said.

Jacob refused to let them take Benjamin. Thinking that his son Joseph was dead, that left only Benjamin of the two sons born of Rachel, his beloved. He just didn't want him to go at that time even though Joseph wanted him to be where he was. ("that where I am, there you may be also" [Jn. 14:3b]).

Jacob didn't know that Joseph was the one dispensing the grain, so he refused to let Benjamin go. Finally Judah, the very one who earlier had the idea to sell Joseph to the Ishmaelites, said he himself would be the surety (ransom) for him, that his father could hold him personally responsible for the safe return of Benjamin. So Judah pledged himself and said,

> ...*We will arise and go, that we may live and not die, we as well as you and our little ones. ... For if we had not delayed, surely by now we could have returned twice* (Genesis 43:8,10).

When they got there and Joseph saw his beloved younger brother (his true blood brother) with the others, he said to his house steward, "Bring the men into the house...and make ready; for the men are to dine with me at noon" (Gen. 43:16b).

They were afraid as they came near to Joseph's house, thinking they might be made slaves, but that wasn't the Joseph way. The steward of the house was at the entrance. He reassured them saying, "The God of your father has given you treasure in your sacks" (See Gen. 43:23). They were worried because of the money they found in their sacks the last time, afraid Joseph would think they stole it. Joseph is a clear type of Jesus. Jesus was also a Jew.

But we have this treasure in earthen vessels, that the surpassing greatness of the power may be of God and not from ourselves (2 Corinthians 4:7).

The brothers were glad Joseph was dealing kindly with them, but they still didn't recognize him as their brother. They were rejoicing in the fact that they were still free.

...Whenever a man turns to the Lord, the veil is taken away. Now the Lord is the Spirit; and where the Spirit of the Lord is, there is liberty (2 Corinthians 3:16-17).

After Joseph's brothers were brought into his house and given water, their feet were washed, and their beasts of burden were given food. They prepared their gift for Joseph's arrival for they had heard about the meal they would be eating with him.

When he came home and had his first glimpse of his younger brother, he was overcome and hurried out seeking a place to weep. He then came out and said, "serve the meal." (Jesus wept over Jerusalem [Lk. 19:41].)

And the Lord of hosts will prepare a lavish banquet for all peoples on this mountain; a banquet of aged wine, choice pieces with marrow and refined, aged wine. And on this mountain He will swallow up the covering which is...over all nations (Isaiah 25:6-7).

They were seated before him, the firstborn according to his birthright and the youngest according to his youth. He took portions from his own table, and the brothers were amazed to see that Benjamin's portion was five times as much as any of theirs.

Chapter 6

Gate to the Camp

Then Moses stood in the gate to the camp, and said, "Whoever is for the Lord, come to me!"... (Exodus 32:26).

In the second book of the Bible, we again find the people making bricks, but not to make a name for themselves as at the Tower of Babel. These people are slaves, forced by Pharaoh to make bricks for the cities he is building in his dynasty.

The Israelites didn't sell themselves into slavery as some Egyptians did. When they first went down to Egypt, it was with great favor because of who Joseph was and because of their relationship to him. He was second only to Pharaoh in power. They were given some of the best land in Goshen. Then things changed when the new pharaoh came, a pharaoh who didn't know Joseph; they came into bondage.

God remembered His promise to Abraham, Isaac, and Jacob, and He wanted to bring them out of the bondage of Egypt into the promised land.

Things went pretty well in Goshen for a time. In as little as ten generations under God's blessings, they grew from a group of a few hundred to a nation of nearly three million. This created fear among the Egyptians, and the new ruler may have resented the favor shown to them by the Pharaoh before him.

At any rate, they suddenly found themselves as a nation of slaves right there in the place of earlier blessings. As Pharaoh sought to control and oppress them, God determined to deliver them. And if ever there was a man who had his work cut out for him, it was Moses. He was faced with the tremendous task of leading this multitude of stubborn, undisciplined slaves out of Egypt and forming them into a nation set apart for God. (Often Egypt is used symbolically in the Bible as a type of the world or its systems.)

The history of the exodus is a story of God's adoption of these Hebrews as His own people, a kingdom of priests, to bring salvation to others. He said they were to be His own possession from among the peoples (see Ex. 19:5).

The Lord certainly knew what a difficult operation it would be to lead them. Therefore He selected a man of great strength, intelligence, and talent for the job. The story of Moses as a baby in the tiny ark made of rushes and reeds is a fascinating beginning to a story that is unequaled in its drama and action.

This future deliverer was born during a time of great distress for Israel. Not only were they enslaved and oppressed but an edict had been prepared that ordered the death of all male babies.

This would certainly have aborted any future plans for leadership among the Hebrews; they were a hardy race, growing in numbers all the time. It was through some creative thinking on the part of Moses' mother that he ended up in the little boat where Pharaoh's daughter found him among the grasses and saved him from death.

His mother hid him at home for three months before she put him in the basket. (The same Hebrew word is used in connection with this basket as was used with reference to Noah's ark.) In God's providence, Moses was placed in a palace in Egypt for the first forty years of his life. There he received instruction from the best educational facilities in the most culturally advanced country of that day.

He was surrounded by luxury after Pharaoh's daughter found him floating in the bullrushes and adopted him. The interesting aspect of this story is that Moses' own mother was called in to nurse the baby and care for the child until he grew to maturity. This mother must have had a tremendous influence on Moses, teaching him of his heritage as a Hebrew while he grew up as a prince in the palace of Egypt. Moses's mother seems to be a symbol of the Holy Spirit in this story.

When Moses came to manhood, he remembered his people and, according to Stephen's discourse before the council in Acts 7, he had already (in his mind) planned their deliverance. When he was approaching the age of forty, it entered his mind to visit his brethren who were in bondage. While he was there he saw one of them being mistreated by an Egyptian. He interceded, and by taking matters into his own hands, killed a man, was seen doing it, and had to flee for his life to Midian where he was an alien.

He was acting ahead of God at that time, moving in his own strength and wisdom rather than in the plan of God. The next forty years were spent in the wilderness. Tending flocks for his father-in-law, Moses undoubtedly experienced a totally different life style. Life was much slower in the wilderness than in Egypt, and his emotions were being tempered by the tedious harshness of the land.

In a twinkling one day, the monotony disappeared. Moses saw a bush that was burning without being consumed. Moses' life would never be the same. A new age was dawning, the Age of the Law.

Moses could have chosen to stay in the palace as a prince, but he chose to identify with his brethren just as the Son of God later chose to do at the dawning of the Age of Grace. ("The Word became flesh and dwelt among us" [Jn. 1:14].) About 1,300 years after Moses, Jesus Christ the Messiah (the Great Deliverer) came to do the work of the Father. He said He would not be ashamed to call us "brethren" (Heb. 2:11). He, like Moses, could have chosen not to do it. He could have stayed in his ivory palace of Heaven, but He "remembered His people" and was willing to come to earth and live in the flesh.

God had gotten Moses' attention with the fire that burned within the bush! After gazing at it, Moses said, "I will turn aside." He knew God had something more important for him to do, something more important than his livelihood of caring for his father-in-law's flocks. He was to be a *deliverer*, so he turned aside to the great task God had put before him. It was a high calling.

Three months after the Hebrews left Egypt, God first spoke to Moses at the wilderness of Sinai. He said,

> *...Go to the people and consecrate them today and tomorrow, and let them wash their garments; and let them be ready for the third day, for on the third day the Lord will come down on Mount Sinai in the sight of all the people* (Exodus 19:10-11).

Later, in the New Testament, Peter gave us a spiritual clue to help us understand endtime prophecy.

> *But do not let this one fact escape your notice, beloved, that with the Lord one day is as a thousand years, and a thousand years as one day* (2 Peter 3:8).

Two thousand years have passed since Jesus came to earth. Is the Church about to enter the third day?

On Mount Sinai at the dawning of the third day, there were flashes of lightning and thunder. A thick cloud descended upon the mountain, and a very loud trumpet sounded, causing all the people in the camp to tremble.

Back when the mixed multitude first left Egypt with all their flocks and herds, the Egyptians were glad to see them go. They couldn't bear to experience any more of the plagues God sent. They gladly complied with any and all requests made by the Hebrews. Moses had instructed them to ask for articles of gold, silver, and clothing. Thus they plundered the Egyptians. They must have acquired some good clothing as it lasted the entire forty years they wandered. Under God's miraculous care and protection their shoes didn't even wear out.

The worst of it is that the trip to Canaan should have been made in a month to six weeks. They had a lot of problems, the same kind we have today. One of the biggest problems was grumbling. They weren't exactly what you would call a well-trained army. Each person had a mind of his own, and they didn't know how to handle their newfound freedom.

This was God's possession—His kingdom of priests? It was always God's desire to have a "called-out" nation unto Himself, a kingdom that He could bless that they in turn might bless the world. But what about this disorderly group? It's like the old saying, "first Moses got the Israelites out Egypt; then Joshua had to get Egypt out of the Israelites." Yes, they had a lot of problems, but God had a plan.

When the Lord visited Sinai, it was a terrifying thing to the people. Bounds were set so they couldn't break through into His presence. Moses was given the Ten Commandments and instructions for the building of the Ark of the Covenant. God said He would meet with them between the wings of the cherubim, above the mercy seat. This was a new thing. Not since Adam had God met with Man on earth.

The Israelites were given instructions for worship down to the last detail. This "new thing" would be a turning point for man. The ark of the Covenant would represent God's presence with him.

There was a time when God's patience wore very thin with the Israelites. When He saw they had made the golden calf, He told Moses He would not go into their midst because they were stubborn, obstinate people and that He was afraid if He went near them for even a moment, He would destroy them.

That's understandable. After all, not only had they seen God provide light at night and shade by day, water from a rock, and manna every morning, but God had actually spoken to them at the mountain. Yet they were so immature, with such a short attention span, they got in trouble when Moses didn't come back as soon as they expected. Moses was on the mountain getting the last of the instructions for the imminent move of God. They already had the plans for the tabernacle and rules concerning the Feasts. Now they were about to get the Ten Commandments.

When the Lord said He was going to destroy the people, Moses begged God to spare them, asking Him to remember His promises to Abraham, Isaac, and Jacob. "So the Lord changed His mind…" (Ex. 32:14).

Then Moses turned and went down from the mountain with the two tablets of the testimony. Joshua joined him, calling his attention to the noise and revelry below centered around the golden calf. God had already seen it and anger burned in Him. God wasn't the only one who was angry; Moses was furious. He threw down the stone tablets that had been written on by the finger of God and broke them. He must have felt those people were, at that point, "non-salvageable."

And he took the calf which they had made and burned it with fire, and ground it to powder, and scattered it over the surface of the water, and made the sons of Israel drink it (Exodus 32:20).

Then Moses stood in the *gate to the camp*, and said, "Whoever is for the Lord, come to me! And all the sons of Levi gathered to him" (Ex. 32:26). He instructed them to "clean house" in the camp, so they took their swords as he said and went back and forth from gate to gate in the camp until about three thousand fell that day. (The New Testament says the Word of God is the "Sword of the Spirit" [Eph. 6:17].)

So the sons of Levi purged the camp, and Moses said they must dedicate themselves to the Lord that very day, and he interceded for the people. (Jesus, in Heaven, intercedes for us today.)

Then the Lord spoke to Moses, "Depart, go up from here" (Ex. 33:1). Much later, God spoke through the prophet Isaiah with a similar command concerning a future move of God in the last days when He would again do something new.

Gate to the Camp

Depart, depart, go out from there, touch nothing unclean; go out of the midst of her, purify yourselves, you who carry the vessels of the Lord (Isaiah 52:11).

This move will come at the end of the age; it was not in the age that Isaiah lived. He prophesied far beyond that to a time to come when the Lord will go forth like a warrior after keeping silent for a long time (see Is. 42:13-14).

I am the Lord, that is My name; I will not give My glory to another, nor My praise to graven images. Behold, the former things have come to pass, now I declare new things. Before they spring forth I proclaim them to you (Isaiah 42:8-9).

When Moses stood in the *gate to the camp* with his eyes blazing, the moment of truth had come. There would be no more disobedience. The plan of God would continue on schedule. They were headed for the promised land.

I can't help believing that the golden calf somehow prefigures something else that will exist in the day that Isaiah was seeing—a future day when people will no longer fear God but will take for themselves another god.

It's hard to imagine what it might be. We have many idols today like money, fame, education, sports, and leisure activities, but the golden calf was an object they had made and were worshiping. I find it difficult to believe that they really thought it was a god after all the signs and wonders Jehovah God had already shown them in the wilderness. Perhaps they simply didn't care one way or the other. Maybe they were bored and wanted a festival to liven things up, whatever it took.

What it did take was a lot of gold, collected and donated by the various individuals in the camp. It would seem that any future fulfillment of the golden calf would require something that generates strong feelings and emotions, such as nationalism, religion, fear, or a combination of all three, something people can rally around with enthusiastic zeal. On the other hand, it might be just the latest edition or rebirth of the old "sacred cows" of the past; there are those that seem immune from criticism, "pillars and asherim" (doctrines and traditions) that were to have been torn down and destroyed at the time of entrance into the promised land.

Chapter 7

Gate of Jericho

...When you hear the sound of the trumpet, all the people shall shout with a great shout; and the wall of the city will fall down flat, and the people will go up every man straight ahead (Joshua 6:5).

Moses received the Ten Commandments and the legal and ceremonial laws. He was given the intricate instructions for the building of the Ark of the Covenant and the tabernacle because God wanted them to learn to worship Him properly. He commanded the Israelites to observe the three main feasts.

The Ark of the Covenant prefigures Jesus. The feasts of the Lord seem to represent our steps toward maturity in Christ.

It would be safe to say that by this point in their wanderings, God's people were totally different from those who began the journey. Strong leadership and discipline kept order while journeying as well as during encampment, but even so, there were still times of rebellion when some challenged Moses' leadership and thousands died in divine judgment.

The harshness and beauty of the wilderness alone would affect a change of character and personality. The rough life they lived as nomads also forced them to depend on God as He tested and toughened them while at the same time miraculously caring for them.

Moses had undergone God's divine process of molding and remaking long before, during his forty years in Midian. He too had to learn God's ways. The solitary life of a shepherd cleared Moses' mind of all the things of the world before God approached him with the commission to deliver His people out of the bondage of Egypt.

Today we understand Egypt to be a type of the "world" or man's systems. God's chosen people went to Egypt to get grain, and they fared very well because of their relationship with Joseph.

Understanding that these Old Testament stories prefigure things to come and that stories of actual events also foreshadow specific endtime happenings, we see a new alignment coming into view. The deliverer is being prepared. The deliverer will come from Zion. A remnant of God's people today have heard His voice, and they follow the Lamb (Jesus) wherever He goes.

They have followed Him out of the bondage of the world system only to find themselves out in the perplexing wilderness, learning God's ways as Moses did.

In the humbling and toughening experience outside the world's system, they are rejected and despised by those within it. Stephen and others in leadership positions in the early Church, encountered similar treatment as one age ended and another began.

Moses had an important job ahead of him and much preparation preceded it. Those back in Egypt must have thought them foolish until they were finally ready to enter the promised land. Returning to the golden calf incident, things started to happen after Moses stood in the gate to the camp. There was a definite separation at that time.

Another separation!

Abraham was separated from Lot; Hagar and Ishmael were separated from Abraham's household; and Jacob and Esau could not live under the same roof with flesh striving against spirit.

After purging the camp, Moses went back up on the mountain, and he asked God to show him His ways and to show him His glory. He got the tablets replaced and the covenant renewed. Things were looking better. Last minute warnings and reminders were given,

1. Make no covenant with the inhabitants of the land.
2. Tear down their altars; cut down their asherim (idols); and smash their sacred pillars (traditions).
3. Observe the Sabbath.
4. All men must observe the three main feasts—Passover, Pentecost, and Tabernacles.

In the three main feasts of the Old Testament, we can see foreshadowed the things to be fulfilled in the New Testament, through Jesus Christ.

The *Feast of Passover*, like the blood on the doorposts in Egypt, looks toward the blood of Jesus. The *Feast of Pentecost*, like the tongues of fire on that day when the Church Age began, points to the baptism of the Holy Spirit through Jesus our Lord. The *Feast of Tabernacles*, which has not yet been fulfilled, points toward our soon, full redemption at the coming of Jesus our *King*.

When Moses came down from the mountain, the glory was shining upon his face so that they had to cover him with a veil. Can you imagine asking God to show you His *glory*?

At that point Moses must have felt he simply could not go on with these people, but he was newly energized after he saw the glory of God.

They spent a year at Mount Horeb (Sinai), and they then were ready to make the last leg of their journey into the promised land. They made it to Kadesh in eleven days and camped there. Things were looking good, except they were having trouble again. The people were longing again for things back in Egypt. Now Moses was criticized by Miriam and Aaron, his sister and brother.

They were very close to their destination, and God wanted to take them in. The tabernacle of Moses was full of rich symbolism. It had three sections in it—like the three feasts and the three decks on Noah's ark. God wanted to take them into the promised land (the symbolic Holy of Holies), which represented God's very presence. They may have been close to their destination, but they did not enter at that time; they lacked faith.

Twelve spies went in to look over the land, but only two came back with a good report. Joshua and Caleb came back with clusters of grapes so heavy they strung them on a pole. They announced, "It truly is a land of milk and honey. Let's go in and take it!" (See Numbers 13:23,30.) They had the proof of the vision.

The other ten spies could see nothing but the giants in the land. In fear and anger they wanted to stone Joshua and Caleb for their enthusasm. In open rebellion the majority ruled, and the people refused to enter the land.

Reviewing Church history, we can see a pattern of sporadic growth—believers advancing and maturing to a certain point then hesitating in fear and unbelief only to slip back from the point of gain.

With Martin Luther we saw the beginning of restoration in the Church. We saw another move forward at the time of John Wesley and the Protestant movement. After that the Church experienced a long dry spell until the great worldwide outpouring of the Holy Ghost at the turn of this century. In a 1948 revival (during the same time the state of Israel came into being), foundations were laid for the eventual harvest at the end of this age.

Like the people who wanted to stone Joshua and Caleb, a large portion of the Church today resents the enthusiasm of the minority, those with the vision to go farther with God, those with the vision to take the land of promise.

When God wanted to destroy the rebellious and unbelieving Israelites, Moses interceded for them. God then decided the final word would be that every person who was over twenty years old at the time of the exodus from Egypt should die in the wilderness. God must have felt that there was no hope for the older generation. All they thought about was the "good old days" in Egypt. They had lost all their vision, and they had forgotten about the bricks and the bondage. Their imaginations, dulled by negativism, could not conceive of anything better. "where there is no vision, the people perish" (Prov. 29:18a KJV).

When God asked the Israelites to posses the land and tear down all the gods, they refused. Therefore God said,

For forty years I loathed that generation, and said they are a people who err in their heart, and they do not know My ways. Therefore I swore in My anger, truly they shall not enter into My rest (Psalm 95:10-11).

Later we will learn more about God's *rest*. The word *Sabbath* means "rest." The apostle Paul discussed this rest at length in the Book of Hebrews.

The covenant made at Sinai set up the government of God, a theocracy, with Moses serving as the earthly representative of God the King. They were now under the *covenant of the Law*.

Moses didn't get to lead them into the promised land. God said,

> ...*Because you have not believed Me, to treat Me as holy in the sight of the sons of Israel, therefore you shall not bring this assembly into the land which I have given them* (Numbers 20:12).

Moses may have been getting tired of wandering around with these people for so long. He remembered that when he *struck* the rock forty years before, he got plenty of water, but God had asked him this time to *speak* to the rock. He apparently didn't think it mattered that much since it had worked forty years ago, but they were in a new time, a new age (of the Law).

So Joshua assumed command (Jesus will lead). That's the Hebrew form of the word. God said to Joshua, "Every place on which the sole of your foot treads, I have given it to you, just as I spoke to Moses" (Josh. 1:3).

The first and toughest obstacle before them in taking the land was Jericho with its impenetrable walls.

Walls can be for protection, as they were at that time, but the walls we have today (they are not necessarily visible) are usually for keeping something or someone in. Sometimes they may also keep them out. In either case, they create separation.

For centuries, God's people have been separated behind denominational walls. In the beginning it was safe and comforting to be associated with like-minded people. Then as time went on, contact with others was lost along with knowledge of truth. The living water was kept contained and began to stagnate. In some cases the protective walls eventually became prison walls, constraining what was within and inhibiting entrance of that which was without.

So Joshua was faced with this powerful, fortress-like walled city of Jericho, which God had asked them to overcome and conquer before they could think about taking the rest of the land.

At the end of three days, the officers in Joshua's army went through the midst of the camp and commanded the people saying,

> ...*When you see the ark of the covenant of the Lord your God with the Levitical priests carrying it, then you shall set out from your place and go after it. However, there shall be between you and it a distance of 2,000 cubits by measure. Do not come near it, that you may know the way by which you shall go, for you have not passed this way before* (Joshua 3:3-4).

It has been almost 2,000 years since Jesus (our Ark) conquered death. He is our pattern from Heaven, and we are keeping our eyes on Him, the author and perfector of our faith (see Heb. 12:2).

This story of Joshua taking the Israelites into the promised land is a foreshadow of our following Jesus into the Holy of Holies beyond the veil.

Jesus did it, so today we press on toward the measure of the stature of the fullness of Christ (see Eph. 4:13), not wanting to stop short of our goal. We don't want to become "bogged down," as the Israelites did when they were so close to their goal.

The two witnesses of Revelation 11 are much like Joshua and Caleb, they too enter the promised land ahead of the rest of Israel and bring back the fruit of the coming age (power, miracles, etc.). They have the proof of the vision.

The priests carrying the ark were to walk into the water and then stand still. When they did that, suddenly they were standing on dry ground and all Israel crossed over on dry ground. Dry ground is a lot different than shifting sand or swampy, stagnant ground. It makes for a much more "solid footing."

Before the seige on the city, the spies had befriended Rahab the harlot who lived on the city wall. She hid the spies in return for the promise that her family would be safe at the invasion of the city. She was assured that if she tied the scarlet ribbon in the window and gathered her family together in the house, they would be safe during the strife. (This brings to mind the Passover night with the blood on the doorposts; the blood was the sign.) We can see that this points to the precious atoning blood of Jesus, which saves us.

Jericho was locked up tight from fear of the Israelites, but God had given them the city. All they had to do was follow His instructions, which were unique to say the least. (Read all about it in Joshua chapter 6.) They marched around the city seven times on the seventh day, carrying seven trumpets. They were told,

...When you hear the sound of the trumpet, all the people shall shout with a great shout; and the wall of the city will fall down flat... (Joshua 6:5).

The most interesting thing about this is that they were commanded to remain silent until the exact time they were told to shout and cause the city to fall. (I'm sure some of you "seekers of truth" with your eagle vision, are getting ahead of me on the symbolisms and fulfillment of this story.)

At the dawning of the "seventh" day, doing as instructed, the mighty "concentrated, united" shout (message) brought down the walls. The *gate of Jericho* could not hold them back. There would no longer be cities with walls separating. They would be one nation, a holy priesthood unto God.

We read much about cities in the Bible, but the two cities we hear the most about are Jerusalem and Babylon. (They are two cities set against each other.) Jerusalem seems to stand for God's true people, and Babylon stands for the opposite—the apostate church or harlot.

This story surely has to do with God's plan concerning all these cities at the culmination of this present age. With the fall of Babylon, God's Kingdom will be established here on earth. King Jesus will sit upon the throne of David in the temple not made with hands.

You also, as living stones, are being built up as a spiritual house for a holy priesthood... (1 Peter 2:5).

This spiritual house will not be made of bricks that are all alike, as in the Tower of Babel, but it will be made of individually unique stones formed, polished, and fitted comfortably together by the hand of God. This is no "wild-eyed" human enterprise; this is no tower or platform purportedly reaching to heaven laden with astrology, sorcery, and the brotherhood of confusion.

No indeed, this temple not made with hands will stand throughout eternity. God doesn't make any junk or counterfeits. His is always the prototype, original and perfect, the one the devil always tries to copy.

Because of the scarlet thread, Rahab and her family were placed outside the city and were spared, just as the family of Lot was placed outside the city of Sodom before the destruction. What a beautiful picture this is for those who are "in Christ" (in the ark), saved by the scarlet blood of Jesus.

Therefore Jesus also, that He might sanctify the people through His own blood, suffered outside the gate. Hence, let us go out to him outside the camp, bearing His reproach. For here we do not have a lasting city, but we are seeking the city which is to come (Hebrews 13:12-14).

"Outside the camp" may not be the most popular or "in" place to be, but it is the safest. We, along with Abraham, are seeking that glorious city of God and nothing compares with that vision.

In Matthew's genealogy we find that Rahab was the mother of Boaz (husband of Ruth) and great-grandmother of King David. Her life was really turned around because of her belief and help at that time.

What a heritage! Rahab went from being a town prostitute by the gate to become the great-grandmother of Israel's greatest King because she believed in the God of Israel and helped His people at a time of great danger.

Moab and Edom were just the opposite; they were always hindering God's chosen people. God reserved judgment upon them. Moab and Edom lay to the east of the Dead Sea, and we know that Esau was called Edom after he lost his birthright to Jacob (Gen. 36:8).

God makes a clear distinction between those who hinder His own and those who help them, as is found in the story of Rahab and in the Book of Esther.

Isaiah's prophecy concerning Edom is indeed grim; God's sword "which is satiated in heaven" will descend for judgment upon Edom in "a day of vengeance," a year of recompense for the cause of Zion. Edom's streams shall be "turned into pitch, and its loose earth into brimstone, and its land shall become burning pitch." (See Isaiah 34:5,9.)

What a picture this presents! Everybody knows that a pitchy stick of wood is the quickest way to start a fire. It burns fast and hot! This brings to mind the tar pits in the valley of Siddim, that the kings of Sodom and Gomorrah fell into while fleeing (see Gen. 14:10).

This pitch found around the Dead Sea and Mesopotamia is believed to be either bitumen or another viscous flammable liquid. Noah used it to make his ark watertight, as did Moses's mother when she placed him in the little ark in the bullrushes. My dictionary says that *bitumen* is any of various mixtures of hydrocarbons and other substances, occurring naturally or obtained by distillation from coal or petroleum, found in asphalt and tar, and used for surfacing roads, and for waterproofing (*American Heritage Dictionary*, Second College Edition [Boston, MA: Houghton Mifflin Co., 1982]).

It sounds like it could be highly flammable in that area of the Middle East, just as Isaiah pictured it. (See Isaiah 34:9.) We pray this is a symbolic description, depicting the fire of God's presence rather than a literal description of missiles igniting the oil fields. Lot no doubt observed a similar sight as he looked from his place of safety as Sodom burned. I am at a loss to imagine any comparative "spiritual" situation fitting the description pictured.

Jericho is near the Dead Sea, but it is on the other side of the Jordan River from Edom. The Jordan definitely is a dividing point in the Old Testament. Edom today would be the Arab country known as Jordan.

Chapter 8

The Gates of Eckron

Prophetically, the story of David prefigures an outstanding endtime event.

The two hundred year period of the judges following Joshua's death was filled with restless turbulence. Problems of idolatry and jealousy between tribes further weakened the nation when it was already oppressed by the Philistines.

Eli had been acting as both priest and judge. He had done a good job, but he was getting old and blind and his sons were a disgrace to the priestly office. He tried to straighten them out, but they were out of control. So the Lord said He would punish them.

The punishment was soon in coming. In a battle with the Philistines, Israel was defeated, and the Ark of God was taken. (Symbolically, the Philistines represent the enemy, the devil.) The glory was departing from Israel (see 1 Sam. 4:21).

Thus a new era began, and God removed His presence from the old order. Samuel judged Israel all the days of his life and the Philistines were subdued during that time. The calling of Samuel was a real turning point for God's people in the Old Testament. It was at this critical time that the ark was taken. In His wisdom, God picked out Samuel. He'd actually been prepared from birth to be brought forward at this time of great need.

In spite of his great success in the prophetic role, when he was old Israel demanded a king. They said to Samuel, "...Behold, you have grown old, and your sons do not walk in your ways. Now appoint a king for us to judge us like all the nations" (1 Sam. 8:5).

This upset Samuel, and he prayed to God to ask Him about it. He knew God was their king (1 Sam. 12:12). God answered Samuel,

> *...Listen to the voice of the people in regard to all that they say to you, for they have not rejected you, but they have rejected Me from being king over them.... Now then, listen to their voice; however, you shall solemnly warn them of the procedure of the king who will reign over them* (1 Samuel 8:7,9).

So Samuel went to the people and spoke God's words to them, effectively saying, "I'll warn you what a king will do for you." In that warning I feel God paints a picture of the future ecclesiastical systems of the world. The items listed as part of the king's procedure appear in First Samuel 8. In essence God said,

"He'll take your offspring and put them in charge of his domain, to run before his own chariots; he'll take a tenth of your vineyards and give them to his servants to do his own work; he'll take a tenth of your flocks, and you yourselves will become his servants" (1 Samuel 8:11-17, my paraphrase). (What an oppressive picture!)

But the people didn't care. They said, "No, but there shall be a king over us (1 Sam. 8:19b). Read it for yourself.

They insisted on a human king to judge them and fight their battles. They wanted to identify with a group and give allegiance to its leader like the other nations, even if it might lead them into brick-making once again as it had at the Tower of Babel.

Man seems to desire to be under authority, but for some reason he rejects God and seeks a man, who invariably puts burdens on him.

When they have something to bite with their teeth [a bit?], *they cry, "Peace," but against him who puts nothing in their mouths, they declare holy war* (Micah 3:5b).

We love to get the bit in our mouths and go, to get the show on the road, to do something even if it's wrong. We feel secure as long as others in our circle are running the same race. We can't *see* God, so in our earthbound state we seek a man and a "place" to worship. Like spoiled children, Israel demanded a human king and all that went with it. It's no secret to any of us that a government formed to serve the people usually ends up with the people serving it.

In answer to the question of where to worship, we have a New Testament example of a woman whose whole life was changed when, after asking Jesus where she should worship, she suddenly "saw" Him! She perceived that He was the Messiah! This Samaritan woman at the well asked of Him,

> *Sir, I perceive that You are a prophet. Our fathers worshipped in this mountain, and you people say that in Jerusalem is the place where men ought to worship* (John 4:19b-20).

Jesus said to her,

> *...Woman, believe Me, an hour is coming when neither in this mountain, nor in Jerusalem shall you worship the Father. ... But an hour is coming, and now is, when the true worshipers shall worship the Father in spirit and truth; for such people the Father seeks to be His worshipers. God is spirit and those who worship Him must worship in spirit and truth* (John 4:21,23-24).

This woman had seen Jesus, and spiritual things were no longer difficult to grasp. Man's tendency is to think the things seen are more real than the unseen things. One day we too shall see Him, and then we won't be seeing in a mirror dimly (see 1 Cor. 13:12).

Just as the people in Samuel's time demanded their king, we today are also short on patience. We like to accomplish things that are seen.

God spelled it out to them, loud and clear through the prophet just what was involved by demanding a king. But they got what they wanted, and God said "tell them that when they cry out in that day because of the king they have chosen, I'll not answer" (see 1 Sam. 8:18).

If the Church is "spiritual" Israel, then symbolically we are living in the time period represented by Saul's reign. We can learn much from this story; we are at the end of his time as king. The glory has departed; the troops are underfed; the enemy is on every side as Saul sleeps under the pomegranate tree (see 1 Sam. 14:2).

Long ago in his immaturity, David was anointed to reign, but most have forgotten all about that happening. He's not been doing much of anything—working out of the mainstream with a few sheep.

As Saul sleeps and his bakers and perfumers are busy turning the wheels of the well-organized kingdom, suddenly there is a great shaking among the people in the camp and all around.

His watchmen see the multitudes dispersing, going here and there. Suddenly Saul springs into action, ordering the people to be counted to see who is gone. His own son is out there with David where the excitement is.

The earlier anointing of David was unusual in that no one expected God to choose someone like him. He was the youngest of Jesse's sons. The others had been in Saul's army long enough to know his ways, and they were respected by all. Everyone knew their works.

Why did God choose David? It was a bitter thing for his older brothers to accept. They probably thought it a mistake. He wasn't the type to be a king; he was too young and not qualified. He wasn't doing anything of any importance, and he hadn't changed in his brother's eyes since his anointing. But David felt different since that time. His heart sang within him in a new joy as he sang unto the Lord and played his harp. The approval of his brethren was of little importance compared to this newfound joy in the Lord. David had to grow to full stature before he began his reign.

Saul had a problem when he awakened. The enemy was upon them, and the people weren't ready. Saul decided they needed the Ark of God, but it wasn't with them. (In the types of the Bible, Jesus is our Ark.)

The noise in the camp of the enemy continued and increased, and by the time Saul's people rallied and came to the battle, every man's sword was against his fellow (see 1 Sam. 14:20).

Confusion and noise reigned. In the battle that followed, the Israelites were hard pressed because of the order Saul had issued; they were not to have any food until the enemy was vanquished (an underfed army?).

Saul's son Jonathan hadn't heard the order, so when he saw a honeycomb in the forest, he eagerly dipped his staff in it and took in the nourishment, his eyes brightening. The people scolded him, reminding him of the oath they'd been placed under, the commitment to Saul's house. Though they were extremely weary and hungry, they were listening to Saul's voice, keeping their eyes on him, and they were not prepared for the battle. They needed their daily bread. Jonathan answered the legalistic "finger-pointers" by saying, "My father has troubled the land" (1 Sam. 14:29). In his youthful zeal, he just reached out for nourishment wherever it was to be found, just as young people might do today.

At one point God regretted making Saul king of Israel. He never was really a good king, even though he was anointed and had experienced a change of heart at the beginning. Among other things that were displeasing to God, Saul's act of disobedience in sparing the life of Agag was his undoing and caused him to lose the kingdom (see 1 Sam. 15:28). Agag was the king of the Amalekites (a symbol of the flesh).

The house of Saul was falling.

Saul admitted he hadn't obeyed God, but rather had listened to the people. Samuel told Agag before he killed him, "Your sword has made women childless." (In biblical types, *women* symbolize churches.) Paul instructed the believers at Ephesus to take "the sword of the Spirit, which is the word of God" (Eph. 6:17). Agag's sword was of flesh (human works).

God would now begin again with the next phase of His plan.

Saul's day was ending; David's was about to begin. This is also where we stand today. David is a type of Jesus. In this story he stands for the Lord's army—His overcoming saints. Saul represents man's religious systems. His day is ending.

After the Spirit of the Lord departed from Saul and his kingdom, he was troubled by an evil spirit that filled him with fear. He called for David to bring his kind of music into the house to soothe his troubled soul. (Music usually helps as numbers decline.)

David had a pretty good idea what was going on between Saul's army and the Philistines (the enemy). He had been watching from the sidelines as he went from his father's house to tend the flocks at Bethlehem. One day his father sent him with some food for his brothers, and he entered the battle lines. While he was there, sure enough the giant from Gath came out and started frightening the men. Some ran.

There were two hills opposite each other. Almost daily the Philistines on one hill spoke brazen lies against the Israelites on the other hill. (If they'd had television then, it would have been on the nightly news.) They had been camped there for forty days when David came on the scene.

He entered the battle lines, sized up the situation, and asked, "What will be done for the man who kills this Philistine and takes away the reproach from Israel? For who is this uncircumcised Philistine, that he should taunt the armies of the Living God?" (1 Sam. 17:26)

This might well be the cry of the believer at the end of the twentieth century in response to the babble of accusations directed against the people of God (the noisy giant presuming to take it upon himself to judge the Church).

David's presence was reported to King Saul, and he sent for him. David told him there was no reason to be intimidated by the giant. He offered to go fight the giant himself, but Saul answered him with words most young men have heard before coming to full manhood, "You can't do this; you are but a youth." In other words, "We've tried it. Certainly if we couldn't do it, you can't."

Finally though, Saul gave his blessings and sent him off.

He was loaded down with Saul's garments and a bronze helmet. They clothed him with armor, but that wasn't David's style. He could barely walk, so he took them off, picked up his slingshot and five smooth stones, and was off to kill the giant Goliath. David represents a chosen generation at the end of this age (God's army), when the hills will again stand as two opposing kingdoms.

David put up with the threats of the sarcastic giant for awhile, then he said,

You come to me with a sword, a spear, and a javelin, but I come to you in the name of the Lord of Hosts, the God of the armies of Israel, whom you have taunted. This day the Lord will deliver you up into my hands, and I will strike you down and remove your head from you…that all the earth may know that there is a God in Israel, and that all this assembly may know that the Lord does not deliver by sword or by spear; for the battle is the Lord's… (1 Samuel 17:45-47).

This battle of all battles will be fought in the realm of the spirit! This present move of God today will bring us into that realm. "Not by might nor by power, but by My

Spirit says the Lord of hosts" (Zech. 4:6b). David was speaking prophecy, speaking words of faith as he advanced toward the enemy. He quickly put a stone in his sling and hit the giant. As the stone sank into the giant's forehead, he fell dead!

The Lord is my rock and my fortress and my deliverer, my God, my rock, in whom I take refuge; my shield and the horn of my salvation, my stronghold (Psalm 18:2).

Thus David prevailed over the enemy, and there was no sword in his hand. He hit him with the rock. He hit him in the forehead, right where the mind is, right at the seat of the problem, the seat of his pride and intellect. They chased the Philistines clear to the *gates of Eckron*, even to Gath (see 1 Sam. 17:52).

The name *Eckron* means extermination, and *Gath* means winepress.

David's fame went before him. The son of Jesse was a hero, and that made Saul angry. He didn't appreciate the little song the women sang as he entered the cities, "Saul has slain his thousands, and David his ten thousands" (see 1 Sam. 18:7).

Saul asked, "What more can he have now but my kingdom?" He could see what was ahead. From that day on he looked upon David with suspicion and jealousy, not understanding God's plan for him. Certainly David did things differently. He had his own way of worshiping God, and it disgusted his wife, the daughter of Saul (see 2 Sam. 6:16). Sons were born to David, but fear was growing in Saul.

There was a long war between the house of Saul and the house of David. David grew steadily stronger, but the house of Saul grew weaker continually (see 2 Sam. 3:1).

Samuel the prophet was dead. The enemy was camped at the border. Saul inquired of the Lord, but He did not answer. So Saul sought a spirit-medium. He was sinking lower in his desperation, having at one time had a genuine anointing, now he did this after the glory departed. Remember that God warned them when they demanded a human king, saying to Samuel, "tell them that when they cry out in that day because of the king they have chosen, I'll not answer" (see 1 Sam. 8:18).

Scripture tells us that the stories about Israel are for our instruction, "...upon whom the ends of the ages have come" (1 Cor. 10:11). That means us, today! Does this story of Saul and David tell us that those that are represented by Saul (man's fleshly church systems) will actually be seeking a spirit-medium after the glory has departed and God no longer answers their prayers? Would it be possible for churches that once had the anointing of God to replace the one true God of Abraham, Isaac, and Jacob with the idols and gods of Babylon? Might Jerusalem (the Church) be once more defeated by the Chaldeans, those noted for their astrology?

To finish the story of David, on the third day he and four hundred of his men pursued the Amalekites victoriously and were dividing the spoils with those who were too tired to go to battle, when they received news of Saul's death. As the Philistines symbolize the enemy, the Amalekites represent the flesh. Amalek was a grandson of Esau, Jacob's twin brother who traded his birthright for a bowl of stew.

The Bible tells us that there is the natural and the spiritual. The spiritual is not first, but the natural, then the spiritual (see 1 Cor. 15:46). In the past we have read much prophetic teachings having to do with the natural (alignment of nations, etc.), which is quite interesting, but in this book we are more concerned with the spiritual.

Satan's time is running out. He's the same old satan, only more desperate; he's the same old serpent with his bag of counterfeits. He has come with his counterfeit religions of the East, along with the rest of the amalgamation of cultic, satanic, and other weirdo "isms" straining to bring in the New Age, including his phony miracles and his phony trinity of man (666). He even stole God's covenant sign, the rainbow. He has his counterfeit messiah poised as if for some great move. He has made elaborate plans for uniting mankind into his kingdom, but he just can't seem get it straight that Jesus won the war at Calvary, and that this is just the mop-up, the occupation.

Satan isn't prepared for the show that God has planned in the very near future, a plan that will put the devil to open shame. He must know that God is preparing a deliverer because he's in the business of killing babies again. When Moses the deliverer was about to be born, he was around killing babies, likewise at the time of Christ's birth when the Messiah (the Great Deliverer) was expected. This, however, is the first time it has ever been done on such a large, worldwide scale—with the mass of abortions being performed today.

Satan's black oil in the Middle East, the power he holds over the nations, cannot compare with God's oil (the symbol of the Holy Spirit). The Holy Spirit in us is the secret that was kept hidden in ages past, the secret that angels wanted to know more about. "Christ in me, the hope of glory" (see Col. 1:27); the new creation having access to both heaven and earth is God's big endtime surprise. It is Jacob's dream of the ladder. This is better than the tower of Babel. We begin to see that in order for there to be counterfeits, there has to be the genuine. And we know that the prototypes come from Heaven.

Digressing a bit into the natural scheme of things, we see the oil (or anointing) of the Holy Ghost produces love, joy, peace, etc., while the black oil of satan has produced hatred, greed, strife, overindulgence, sorcery, idolatry, and so on. This oil will never unite Ishmael's Arab nations. The only thing that could ever unite them is their hatred of Israel and their desire to possess Jerusalem, forcibly pushing Isaac out of the picture. These brothers just do not get along.

No, God's covenant will not be established through Ishmael, son of the bondwoman "for the son of the bondwoman shall not be an heir with the son of the free woman" (Gal. 4:30b). The apostle Paul explained that these two women represent two covenants and therefore have a bearing upon our beliefs today.

This ongoing battle, the battle that is heating up in intensity during our times, will eventually evolve into the battle of the ages. However, it will come to a quick halt when the King of kings and Lord of lords comes with his spiritual army, those who are His chosen and anointed people. When King Jesus sets up His Kingdom here on earth, Ishmael and Esau will not be part of the inheritance.

This was the saddest aspect of the story of David and King Saul; Jonathan just went along with things, hoping they might get better. He did not want to be disloyal to his father Saul. He knew David had been secretly anointed to be king, and although he knew that he, as Saul's son, stood to inherit the kingdom, he still lived for the day when he would stand beside David in God's new kingdom. As a boy, he had even given David his robe, visualizing him as king.

Unfortunately, it didn't happen that way. Jonathan was always trying to reconcile Saul and David, and somehow he never got around to leaving Saul's house. Instead of being with David in the new kingdom, he fell in disgrace with his father Saul in battle. Jonathan was killed, and Saul committed suicide. (The spiritual is not first, but the natural, then the spiritual [1 Cor. 15:46]) Most of us can see ourselves or others in this colorful story, but still it is hard for us to grasp this connection between the natural and spiritual, even though Paul explained it two thousand years ago.

As we see the nations lining up in the Middle East, we can be sure that the spiritual counterpart (the

Church), will be affected as well. There has been a separation taking place within the Church. Now, as then, the flesh strives against the spirit (see Gal. 4:29).

Before David came to the throne, his fondest dream was to bring the Ark of the Covenant home to Jerusalem. He finally brought it to Mt. Zion and put it in a tent. (The apostle Paul also likened our body to a tent: "...Do you not know that your body is a temple of the Holy Spirit, who is in you?" [1 Cor. 6:19a]).

For some reason David was inspired to take the ark to Zion and put it in a tent, rather than to the *tabernacle of the congregation* at Gibeon, where most of the people were worshiping. The worshipers at Gibeon had the other vessels of the tabernacle, minus the ark, symbolizing Jesus. At the same time David and his little band had the ark, minus the other vessels. (Think about that for a moment. The ark was the place where God said he would meet with man on earth.) God was doing something new at that time, just as He's doing today!

Chapter 9

Outside the Gate

The Age of the Law was closing, just as the Age of the Patriarchs ended with the giving of the Law. The patriarchs had taken them from the Abrahamic Covenant to the Mosaic Covenant. Israel was now looking for their Messiah, and they desperately needed a savior.

John the Baptist had been preaching for some time, preparing the way for the Messiah. John was of priestly descent on both sides of his family. His father Zacharias was a priest, and his mother Elizabeth was a descendant of Moses' brother Aaron.

Despite this fact, John had to go outside the city to preach the message God had given him, a message that was not well received by the Pharisees and Sadducees; they were the religious leaders of that day in Jerusalem. John was proclaiming the coming Messianic Age and the need to be spiritually prepared for it. He proclaimed the need to be able to recognize and accept the Messiah when He appeared.

Multitudes of the common people went out to hear John, and many Jews were baptized. But the priests within the city opposed him because his message was in conflict with their traditional teaching. The Pharisees prided themselves on knowing every "jot and tittle" of the Law.

They were looking for a deliverer all right, but a different type. They sought someone to politically deliver them from their enemies. John was preaching repentance and water baptism for the remission of sin. The Pharisees didn't feel they needed to be baptized because they were descendants of Abraham. They felt that qualified them for the Kingdom.

Baptism didn't seem particularly strange to the ones who came to hear John because the Pharisees had washing and cleansing rituals as part of their introduction into the religion. But those rituals were for gentiles, yet here was John telling the people that they too must repent and be baptized. That was shocking to Pharisees since they were the ones who interpreted the Law. This was a definite departure from what they taught. John the Baptist explained that his water baptism was only a preparation for the Baptism of the Holy Ghost (see Mt. 3:11).

Along with the crowds of common people who came from Jerusalem and Judea, there were some Pharisees who came for baptism. John must have felt they weren't sincere or repentant because he railed at them and called them a "brood of vipers." He said,

As for me, I baptize you with water for repentance, but He who is coming after me is mightier than I, and I am not fit to remove His sandals; He will baptize you with the Holy Spirit and fire (Matthew 3:11).

In his uncompromising sermon John shouted, "Every tree therefore that does not bear good fruit is cut down and thrown into the fire (Mt. 3:10b).

Although he was Jesus' cousin, it appears that John may not have know who he was announcing until shortly before Jesus' baptism. The next day he was still amazed as he spoke to some followers beside him who were staring at Jesus. He said,

Behold, the Lamb of God who takes away the sin of the world! This is He on behalf of whom I said, "After me comes a Man who is higher in rank that I, for He existed before me" (John 1:29b-30).

And the people left John and followed Jesus (see Jn. 1:37). John knew he must decrease and Jesus must increase (Jn. 3:30).

Jesus was born in a blaze of glory. Angels appeared to the shepherds. Magi followed the star to Bethlehem. Simeon prophesied as he spoke to Mary the mother of Jesus, "Behold, this Child is appointed for the fall and rise of many in Israel, and for a sign to be opposed" (Lk. 2:34b).

Simeon had received a revelation by the Holy Spirit that he would not see death before he had seen the Messiah. Therefore he came by the Spirit to the temple where Mary and Joseph had taken the baby Jesus. As he held the baby and spoke the prophecy over Him, he was thrilled to see God's promise had come to pass.

After the excitement caused by His birth, Jesus grew up in obscurity, except for the incident in the temple when He was twelve. Jesus had gone to Jerusalem with His parents for the Passover. When He stayed behind in the temple after His parents left, they returned looking for Him. When questioned, He just said, "…Did you not know I had to be in My Father's house?" (Lk. 2:49)

This was a foreshadow of the Passover that was to be celebrated at the very time He Himself became the fulfillment of the *Feast of Passover*, when His blood was shed for our sins. Afterward, He went to His Father's house in Heaven.

Jesus knew He would fulfill the Passover. He also knew that the times are in the Father's hands. The apostle Paul later wrote,

> *But when the fulness of the time came, God sent forth His Son, born of a woman, born under the Law, in order that He might redeem those who were under the Law, that we might receive the adoption as sons* (Galatians 4:4-5).

John's baptism wasn't enough. It was just the preparation for the rest of what was to come through the Messiah; the goal was redemption and adoption as sons (see Rom. 8:23). Just like the Jewish father, at the time of his son's Bar Mitzvah, when he says to the community, "This is my son and I'm proud of him; and I'll stand behind him on whatever he undertakes," God also spoke of His Son Jesus at the Jordan introduced Him to the world.

Before Jesus came to the Jordan River that memorable day, John quoted from the prophets Isaiah and Malachi concerning his mission and the coming of the Messiah: "Behold, I am going to send My messenger before your face, who will prepare the way; the voice of one crying in the wilderness, 'Make ready the way of the Lord; make His paths straight!' " (see Is. 40:3; Mt. 3:3; Mal. 3:1)

John was pointing out that *he* was that messenger. All Jerusalem was going out to him—*outside the gate*. The scribes and Pharisees had been questioning him, asking, "Are you Elijah the prophet, and if not, then who?" They knew the words of the prophets, and they were expecting Elijah.

Behold, I am going to send you Elijah the prophet before the coming of the great and terrible day of the Lord. And he will restore the hearts of the fathers to their children, and the hearts of the children to their fathers, lest I come and smite the land with a curse (Malachi 4:5-6).

They couldn't see the difference between these Scriptures. There seems to be two Elijah appearances. The Scriptures are very similar, but the great and terrible day of the Lord has not as yet arrived. Like us, they wanted to lump them together and have things come to pass sooner. The first Scripture, from Isaiah, was in reference to John the Baptist at the beginning of the Age of

Grace. The other Scripture from Malachi is to be fulfilled at the end of this age, before the day of the Lord when He comes to establish His Kingdom here on earth. The first prophecy with John the Baptist was ushering in Jesus the Messiah and the Age of Grace, while the last prophecy was a reference to the messenger who would usher in the Kingdom Age.

We are living in that day, yet this is not easy for us to grasp, nor was it easy for those living at the beginning of this age.

In the confusion over their expectations of the Messiah, they concluded that John the Baptist might be the Christ. John assured them he was not, but that he was preparing the way. His water baptism for remittance of sin was part of the preparation for the Christ.

He must have been a sight in his camel hair garments. He lived in the desert, eating honey and wild locusts. No doubt he was a curiosity, lambasting Herod the King and calling the Pharisees and Sadducees a "brood of vipers" (Mt. 3:7). Imagine blasting the chief priests who were highly respected in the city; they were among his priestly relatives. He was preaching, "Repent, for the Kingdom of Heaven is an hand" (Mt. 3:2).

Jesus had been quietly growing in wisdom and stature in the carpenter's shop in Nazareth. Except for the incident in the temple when He was twelve, we don't read much about Him in His early life. Probably most of the people had forgotten about the prophecy at His birth amid all of the other commotion. They may have decided He wasn't the long-awaited Messiah after all.

To the people of Nazareth, I'm sure He was just the carpenter's son. After all, thirty years had gone by.

Then one day when John was baptizing in the Jordan River, Jesus, as a mature man, came up to John and asked to be baptized. Can you picture it? His cousin was asking to be baptized, and the Holy Spirit had alerted John at some point that Jesus was the Messiah because John tried to avoid it.

But John tried to prevent Him, saying, "I have need to be baptized by You, and do You come to me?" But Jesus answering said to him, "Permit it at this time; for in this way it is fitting for us to fulfill all righteousness." Then he permitted Him (Matthew 3:14-15).

Jesus came up from the water immediately after His baptism in front of all John's followers.

And behold, the heavens were opened, and he [John] *saw the Spirit of God descending as a dove, and coming upon Him* [Jesus] *and behold, a voice out of the heavens, saying, "This is My beloved Son, in whom I am well-pleased"* (Matthew 3:16b-17).

Imagine! God spoke in the hearing of them all. How would you like to be announced by God?

What an extraordinary moment! The trinity of God—the Father spoke, the Holy Ghost descended, and Jesus was confirmed as the Son of God by God Himself. At that moment, Jesus received the complete anointing and fullness of the Spirit, yet He still suffered *outside the gate.*

Therefore Jesus also, that He might sanctify the people, through His own blood, suffered outside the gate (Hebrews 13:12).

Yes, Jesus suffered on the cross *outside the gate* of the city, where all the men walked by and could see His shame. Even before that He had to preach His gospel of the Kingdom outside the city; His message wasn't received within the walls of the city. There the established Jewish religious leaders were in power. His message was at odds with the teaching of the hierarchy in Jerusalem. God's timing had come, but they were not ready for such change. Nevertheless, God's plan would move forward, whether or not they moved with it.

Hence, let us go out to Him outside the camp, bearing His reproach. For here we do not have a lasting city, but we are seeking the city which is to come (Hebrews 13:13-14).

Here again is Abraham's city, the one we are looking for.

The people in Jerusalem in Jesus' day, loved their temple worship, the washings, and the burnt offerings. Admittedly, these laws and rituals were hard to perform, but they were what they were familiar with. This was what their fathers had done, and it was all they knew.

From childhood, they had heard their parents and grandparents talk of the coming Messiah. Down through the centuries His coming had been yearned for, but could it be a reality? Could this man who was reading from the scroll of Isaiah really be the Messiah? There was nothing spectacular about this Jesus.

It's easy enough for us to think about things in the future or to reflect upon the past, but these people happened to be living at the time this great prophecy was fulfilled. That kind of a time is usually hard to accept; it's a time of confusion. Things never happen the way they are expected. The people expected Elijah.

Jesus plainly told His disciples that Elijah would come (future) and that actually he had already come, referring to John the Baptist (Mt. 11:3-14). There will be a spirit of judgment connected with the ministry of this endtime messenger. The forerunner of the Day of the Lord, like John the Baptist, will operate in the spirit and power of Elijah (see Lk. 1:17).

The temple worship was still going on even though Jesus had come, bringing with Him the new dispensation. The Age of the Law was ending, and the Age of Grace was beginning.

Walking about in a humble way, Jesus changed the whole course of civilization in His three short years of ministry. He healed the sick, caused the blind to see, changed water into wine, and raised the dead.

For the Son of Man has come to save that which was lost [in Eden] (Matthew 18:11).

With the New Covenant and through the finished work on the cross of Calvary, Jesus made a way for us into the very presence of God once more, the place where Adam and Eve were in the beginning. Jesus fulfilled all righteousness (see Mt. 3:15).

The apostle Paul said,

> *Which [God] brought about in Christ, when He raised Him from the dead, and seated Him at His right hand in the heavenly places, far above all rule and authority and power and dominion, and every name that is named, not only in this age, but also in the one to come* (Ephesians 1:20-21).

What a position! No one can ever be seated higher than that. He is the King of kings and Lord of lords, throughout eternity.

For us, the first step toward his presence is the acceptance of Jesus as Savior. God's grace is extended to "whosoever will," through the sacrificial blood atonement. We come with our sins, just the way we are, to be washed by the blood of the Lamb (Jesus). We don't have to do anything. There's nothing on earth we can do to become worthy of His grace. His grace is sufficient (see 2 Cor. 12:9).

> *...I am the way, and the truth, and the life; and no one comes to the Father, but through Me* (John 14:6).

It's hard to comprehend all that He *Is* and all that He did for us. He is the Resurrection and the Life (Jn. 11:25). He is truly everything to all people!

> *What is man, that Thou dost take thought of him? And the son of man, that Thou dost care for him?* (Psalm 8:4)

Man is, and always has been, searching for truth. He's really concerned about life and the purpose for it. Jesus had all the answers; He *is* the answer (no matter what the problem is). He is the Way. My Bible has a cyclopedic index that lists more than 275 names applied to Christ, for example, Prince of Peace, Son of God, Savior, Lord of glory, Alpha and Omega, Ancient of Days, and Almighty God. It's staggering!

In the last book of the Bible Jesus says, "Behold, I stand at the door and knock; if anyone [singular] hears My voice and opens the door, I will come in to him, and I will dine with him… (Rev. 3:20). (On the road to Emmaus, as it was getting toward evening, the two disciples who had not yet recognized Jesus suddenly had their eyes opened. They recognized Him when He reclined at the table with them, blessed the bread, and began giving it to them (see Lk. 24:30). Please think about the spiritual significance of this.

We surely won't want to turn down Jesus' invitation to come in and dine with Him (see Rev. 3:20). What a shame! In that Scripture, Jesus is talking to the endtime Laodicean church (the wealthy, lukewarm church), and He's standing alone outside the door.

He's probably wondering if anyone hears Him amid the bustling activity of their works. No one opens the door. Do they refuse His dinner invitation, or do they just not hear? The invitation is singular, not congregational.

Immediately after Jesus was baptized in the Jordan River, He was led by the spirit into the wilderness where He fasted forty days. Then He was tempted by the devil. (See Luke 4:1-14.)

That's about as long as one can go without food, and He was tempted every way possible. Satan offered Him food. He offered Him all the kingdoms of the world if He would just bow down and worship him instead of God. He even quoted Scripture to try to trip Jesus up in His weakened state.

In his effort to get Jesus to commit suicide, the devil said, "For it is written, 'He will give His angels charge concerning You to guard You'" (Lk. 10; see also Ps. 91:11).

In other words, the devil was saying, "Now look, we all know You are something special; nothing could hurt You. You could call for angels to help You. Just jump. It will be thrilling!"

But all three times Jesus simply answered the devil with Scripture. He never became confused in His hunger and exhaustion. Afterward, He returned to Galilee in the power and fullness of the Spirit—teaching, healing, and performing all types of miracles.

When Jesus chose His disciples, He just said "follow Me." He didn't say, "go to Jerusalem to the teachers of the Law and inquire as to which of the Rabbi's are the most qualified of men, and study with them for three years." He just said, as to Simon Peter and his brother Andrew, "follow Me and I will make you become fishers of men." And they immediately left their nets and followed Him. (See Mark 1:17-18.)

He didn't send His disciples anywhere else to be taught. He taught them Himself in a very short time. His entire ministry only lasted three and a half years.

His manner of preaching would have been the talk of Galilee—gathering people on hillsides, preaching from boats, multiplying food for a picnic with five thousand people. They'd seen nothing like it before, since they were used to the formal ritual of the temple in Jerusalem.

Jesus was out and about with the people. He went anywhere they were to be found. They had many questions to ask, such as "Why is He eating and drinking with tax gatherers and sinners?" Upon hearing this question Jesus said to them, "It is not those who are healthy who need a physician, but those who are sick; I did not come to call the righteous, but sinners. " (See Mark 2:16-17.)

He explained that you cannot put new wine in old wineskins; the new wine will burst the skins. Similarly, one does not sew in a new piece of material onto an old garment, for if you do, the new will tear away and won't match the old. (See Matthew 9:16-17.)

He was trying to tell them that the new covenant was completely new and not the covenant of the Law patched up to fit the times. He began preaching in their synagogues and was praised by all. The people loved the fresh new teaching, but He upset the religious leaders as He condemned the system of the scribes and Pharisees and taught new doctrine. They called Jesus a blasphemer for not sticking to the letter of the Law. But He said, "Do not think that I came to abolish the Law or the Prophets; I did not come to abolish, but to fulfill" (Mt. 5:17).

He told the multitudes who listened to enter by the strait (narrow) gate.

Enter by the narrow gate; for the gate is wide, and the way is broad that leads to destruction, and many are those who enter by it. For the gate is small, and the way is narrow that leads to life, and few are those who find it (Matthew 7:13-14).

He was trying to show them the way. Israel was in trouble. Their needs were great. The early Christians, before they were first called by that name at Antioch, were called "The people of the Way."

The early Church was acquainted only with the earthly aspects of the Kingdom. They had trouble understanding the spiritual side, and they asked Jesus questions about who would be the most prominent in the Kingdom, etc. Evidently they thought of it more in terms of a military or a political kingdom, one that would destroy the Roman tyranny.

Today, we (taking Christendom as a whole) have quite the opposite problem, for we can't seem to grasp the idea of a spiritual kingdom here on earth with God's will being done "on earth, as it is in heaven" (see Mt. 6:11). We see the world getting worse, and we don't know what to think. At best we have some hazy fairy-tale picture in our minds concerning the "sweet by and by"; we lack any scriptural foundation that would lead us into truth. The excitement of God's wonderful plan for the establishment of His Kingdom here on earth has not been given to most of us. Many question, "Maybe it will be when we get to Heaven?"

With this vague concept of the Kingdom being so widespread, when it is taught any other way it is upsetting to many. It has been a sort of "no touch" subject. People are encouraged to think, "What does it matter? The Kingdom is somewhere up in Heaven and let's just leave it at that."

The truth is, there has been precious little teaching of any kind about the Kingdom in our day. When answering the disciples as to what would be the signs of His coming and of the end of the age, Jesus said,

And this gospel of the kingdom shall be preached in the whole world for a witness to all the nations, and then the end shall come (Matthew 24:14).

I would imagine it has always been a time of confusion, anger, and accusation as one dispensation ended and a new one began; there are always many changes. During the Patriarchal Age, God dealt directly with individuals. During the Age of the Law, He dealt with a group of people as a "called-out" nation. Then along came John the Baptist and the dispensation of grace, with (of all things) something called the Church. That was also a whole new thing.

Each time God does something new, it is met with opposition and outrage. Always there are some people who don't recognize the hand of God in the changes because they are so different from what they've known.

The Israelites had their tabernacle. Later the Jews had their temple and a system that they enjoyed, and they wanted to continue in the same way. Years after Jesus' resurrection, the Jews were still worshiping in the temple. This was long after Pentecost and the beginning of the Church. In A.D. 70 God allowed Titus to burn the temple, thus ended the era of temple worship and animal sacrifice. "He takes away the first in order to establish the second" (Heb. 10:9b).

Chapter 10

The Narrow Gate

When Jesus entered the synagogue on the Sabbath, someone handed Him the scroll of the prophet Isaiah. He opened it to Isaiah 61, a Scripture familiar to everyone. He read,

The Spirit of the Lord is upon Me, because He anointed Me to preach the gospel to the poor. He has sent Me to proclaim release to the captives, and recovery of sight to the blind, to set free those who are downtrodden, to proclaim the favorable year of the Lord (Luke 4:18; see also Isaiah 61:1-2a).

When He finished reading, with all eyes fixed on Him, He closed the book and announced, "Today this Scripture has been fulfilled in your hearing" (Lk. 4:21b). He had stopped reading before He got to the next part of the passage, which reads,

...And the day of vengeance of our God; to comfort all who mourn in Zion, giving them a garland instead of ashes, the oil of gladness instead of mourning, the mantle of praise instead of a spirit of fainting... (Isaiah 61:2-3).

That last part will be fulfilled later, at the end of this age.

The writer of the Book of Hebrews points out that if the Law had been sufficient, Jesus would not have had to come with the New Covenant. But since the Law only made man aware of his sins without any solution, man saw that it was impossible to keep the Law, and he was left with his frustration and "dead works" (Heb. 8:7; Gal. 3:24-26).

Like Moses who could have chosen to stay and live in the palace in Egypt but instead chose to identify with his people, Jesus also chose to leave His place of glory with the Father in order to identify with man in the flesh, with all his trials and temptations.

In doing so, not only could Jesus understand our nature and problems, but He was also able to give us some sort of picture of the nature of God Almighty. The apostle Paul said, "And He is the image of the invisible God, the first-born of all creation" (Col. 1:15). "But [Christ] emptied Himself, taking the form of a bondservant, and being made in the likeness of men" (Phil. 2:7).

He was God manifest in the flesh!

For God sent not His Son into the world to condemn the world; but that the world through Him might be saved (John 3:17 KJV).

The world needed a savior. The Law couldn't save, but it was part of the education and preparation for the coming of Messiah.

Jesus preached to multitudes, sent out seventy disciples, and chose twelve apostles. However, only three men had the privilege of ascending the mountain with Him to witness the glorious sight of His transfiguration. (According to the *American Heritage Dictionary*, *transfiguration* means "a radical transformation of figure or appearance, metamorphosis.")

When Moses ascended the mountain, he let only Aaron go part way. I doubt that Peter, James, and John, those closest to Jesus, had any idea what was about to happen when Jesus took them to the mountain where His body changed before their eyes: "...and His face shone like the sun, and His garments became as white as light, and behold, Moses and Elijah appeared...with Him" (Mt. 17:2-3).

Imagine!

Think about it. One of these days the mountain of the Lord will once again be ascended (see Is. 30:29-30). The festival will be kept. The *Feast of Tabernacles* will be celebrated, and the world will be blessed. A nation will be born in a day. This is the same holy nation that God had in mind when He approached Abraham, a nation that God could bless that its members, in turn, might bless the world. God's plan is right on course and right on time.

Peter wasn't just babbling when he suggested on the Mount of transfiguration that they build booths. He was on the right track. He knew it had something to do with the *Feast of Tabernacles*. Jesus shared many things privately with the twelve. More than likely He explained how He Himself would be the fulfillment of the *Feasts of the Lord*: The *Feast of Passover* was fulfilled through His blood; the *Feast of Pentecost* was fulfilled by the sending of the blessed Holy Spirit; and *Feast of Tabernacles* still awaits fulfillment (of which we within the Body of Christ still await). Try to imagine the fulfillment and the glory accompanying it. It will be a great surprise to many people who haven't yet a hint of what's ahead.

Even at this moment "...the anxious longing of the creation waits eagerly for the revealing of the sons of God" (Rom. 8:19). Our world stands paralyzed with problems and pain, and we are helpless in our rhetoric. We sense that surely these must be the times in which the Lord will return.

The stories in the Bible are for our instruction, so we ponder the significance of this New Testament story about Jesus' transfiguration and the appearance of Moses and Elijah who had been dead for so long. What is to be learned from it?

The things in the Old Testament were mere shadows of things to come, the substance belonging to Christ (see Col. 2:17). The apostle Paul reminded the believers of this:

Who serve a copy and shadow of the heavenly things, just as Moses was warned by God when he was about to erect the tabernacle; for, "See," He says, "That you make all things according to the pattern which was shown you on the mountain" (Hebrews 8:5).

Jesus is the fulfillment of the tabernacle and the Ark of the Covenant. He is our pattern from Heaven. We are to become "conformed" to His image. He was the *firstborn* of many brethren (Rom. 8:29). Can you imagine what this means? Just think about it. He said he would not be ashamed to call us "brethren." That makes us part of God's household—His sons. (See Hebrews 2:11.)

For all who are being led by the Spirit of God, these are sons of God (Romans 8:14).

We can be sure that the transfiguration scene was not merely a foreshadow of what was about to happen to Jesus, for if He is our pattern, it also has something to do with us. Keeping in mind that Jesus took only the three people closest to Him when He went to the mountain, we wonder, "Will it be repeated? Might we be among those who ascend with Him?"

Who may ascend into the hill of the Lord? And who may stand in His holy place? (Psalm 24:3)

We hurry to our Bibles to once again read the seven promises to the overcoming saints that are written in the first three chapters of the Book of Revelation. Straining our minds and our faith to comprehend these things of the spirit, we begin to grasp just a small bit of what Jesus did, who He is, and what our inheritance might be. May His name be praised forevermore! What a mighty God we serve!

Is there any significance in the aspects of the whiteness and "shining" on the Mount of Transfiguration? Imagine the resurrection power present at that moment when the "Voice" out of the cloud said "This is My beloved Son. Hear Him!" (See Matthew 17:5.)

Arise, shine; for your light has come, and the glory of the Lord has risen upon you. For behold, darkness will cover the earth, and deep darkness the peoples; but the Lord will arise upon you, and His glory will appear upon you (Isaiah 60:1-2).

*And many of those who sleep in the dust of the ground will awake, these to everlasting life, but the others to disgrace and everlasting contempt. And those who have insight will **shine** brightly like the brightness of the expanse of heaven, and those who lead the many to righteousness, like the stars forever and ever* (Daniel 12:2-3).

Even the apostles didn't really understand the Kingdom Jesus came to establish; because after He was arrested, "...all the disciples left Him and fled" (Mt. 26:56).

He appeared to certain people after His resurrection and talked with them. This included the night when the disciples were meeting together with the door locked for fear of the powerful Jewish religious leaders. Jesus suddenly "appeared" in their midst (Jn. 20:19). He manifested Himself again (made Himself visible) to His disciples at the Sea of Tiberias (Jn. 21:1).

He inaugurated the redemption plan. The Roman soldiers took Him to the cross where He gave His life for our sins. He then rose from the dead on the third day—to the amazement of most of the people, including the disciples.

He overcame the world, the flesh, and the devil.

The work Jesus came to do was accomplished when just before He died on the cross, He said, "It is finished" (Jn. 19:30).

He made a way for us, and He demonstrated it. He *is* the way!

Since it was finished (completed), He rose from the grave and after appearing to numerous people during a forty day period, He ascended to Heaven in a cloud. He is now there seated at the right hand of the Father.

Jesus didn't appear to everyone during the forty days. Peter said to Cornelius and his assembly at Caesarea,

God raised Him on the third day, and granted that He should become visible, not to all the people, but to witnesses who were chosen beforehand by God, that is, to us, who ate and drank with Him after He arose from the dead (Acts 10:40-41).

He appeared to God's "chosen" witnesses, those with whom He had been eating and drinking after He rose from the dead. That certainly sounds strange, but the men (angels) mentioned in Chapter 4 of this book who appeared to Abraham just before the destruction of Sodom had a meal with him that included meat.

Earlier, while preaching north of Galilee at Caesarea Phillipi, Jesus asked His disciples, "Who do people say the Son of Man is?" They explained that some were saying He was John the Baptist, some thought Elijah; others said Jeremiah or one of the other prophets. But when Jesus pressed them and asked who they themselves thought He was, Simon Peter spoke up, as with a sudden revelation, "Thou art the Christ, the Son of the living God" (Mt. 16:16b).

Jesus knew God had spoken to Peter; He answered him by saying,

Blessed are you, Simon Barjona, because flesh and blood did not reveal this to you, but My Father who is in heaven. And I also say to you that you are Peter, and upon this rock I will build My church; and the gates of Hades shall not overpower it (Matthew 16:17b-18).

Christ would build His Church on the Rock (which is Jesus Himself) and the other living stones of the temple who, like Peter, are tuned in to the things of God, listening for His voice, and receiving revelation knowledge (see 1 Pet. 2:5). Jesus will build His Church. *We* can't build it because we *are* the Church.

While standing at the headwaters of the Jordan several years ago at Banias Springs, which is Caesarea Phillipi of the Bible, I was awed by the beauty. There in that breathtaking setting, I also remembered Jesus' words to Peter.

There the water bubbles out of the rock. Early in the season it cascades over a wide span of flat rock. The

The Narrow Gate

immense rock bluff stands above like a sentinel. The water brings life to the whole valley.

What a picture this presents. Jesus sees each of us (His Church) as living waters in a thirsty land, bubbling out from the Rock (Jesus Christ). He could see in Peter a strength to stand guard over the precious waters flowing out to refresh the dry land.

Right after that, Jesus gave the disciples the keys to the Kingdom, which involves authority to both bind and loose (see Mt. 16:19).

Jesus explained that someday the Son of Man would come in the glory of His Father with His angels and His rewards.

Truly I say to you, there are some of those who are standing here who shall not taste death until they see the Son of Man coming in His kingdom (Matthew 16:28).

Of course, that happened when He triumphed over death, returned from the grave in resurrection power, ascended to the Father, then returned to the midst of His apostles, and sent the Holy Spirit to them fifty days later on the Day of Pentecost.

This proved once and for all who Jesus was—that He was who He said He was and that He lives today. After achieving all that He set out to do, He received back the glory, and He is sitting now at the right hand of the Father.

What an amazing thing! It is hard for us to grasp what really happened in that short time period—how much He did for us and for the whole world.

If John the Baptist preached that the Kingdom of Heaven was at hand, and Jesus made statements like that in Matthew 16:28, then what happened? Why hasn't the Kingdom come to the earth?

Jesus taught the disciples to pray "Thy kingdom come, Thy will be done on earth as it is in heaven" (Mt. 6:10). Men have been praying that prayer for nearly two thousand years, sometimes by rote not even thinking of what they're saying. Has it happened? Have you wondered about it? Did we "drop the ball" or something?

When Jesus appeared to those certain believers after His resurrection, He asked them not to be troubled when He left, because He would prepare a place for them, that where He was going they might also go. He explained to them there are "many dwelling places in His Father's house" (Jn. 14:2).

He instructed His followers not to leave Jerusalem, but to wait for the promise of the Father, the promise they heard when Jesus said to them,

For John baptized with water, but you shall be baptized with the Holy Spirit, not many days from now (Acts 1:5).

One hundred and twenty of His faithful followers were gathered as one in the upper room during the festivities of the Jewish *Feast of Pentecost*. They were waiting for the fulfillment of the promise that they would receive the Holy Ghost. These people were no longer doubters.

They probably wondered what the Holy Ghost might be. No doubt they discussed it among themselves, wondering what the manifestation would be, and how they would know when they had received it.

They needn't have wondered about that. Because to that quiet prayer room, apart from the noise and revelry outside, there suddenly came the noise of a mighty rushing wind that filled the room. There were tongues of fire coming down and touching each of them, "and they were all filled with the Holy Spirit and began to speak with other tongues, as the Spirit was giving them utterance" (Acts 2:4).

Those early believers rushed out from that prayer meeting into the streets of Jerusalem. People were gathered there from all the various countries for the weeklong celebration of the *Feast of Pentecost*. The power and glory came down, and they were speaking unknown languages that those from other countries could understand in their own tongues (just the opposite of what happened at the Tower of Babel). The world of their day was turned upside-down; they healed the sick, cast out demons, and preached the good news of the Kingdom.

While in Jerusalem during a modern *Feast of Tabernacles* celebration, it suddenly hit me that one of these days, the spiritual fulfillment of this feast will come to pass with real live people like you and me right here on earth.

The Jewish Feast of Pentecost was being celebrated the very week that the Church began. The 120 believers, who later became the early Church, were not part of the noise and revelry outside. They were in the upper room, praying and waiting for the promise. They had a vision of something more. The Church was an outgrowth of the Law, and *Tabernacles* will be an outgrowth of the Church.

Just as the *Feast of Passover* was fulfilled when Jesus hung on the cross outside the city while preparations were being made inside the city for that feast, you can surely believe that this third and last great *feast* will come to fulfillment as well while the Jews are in the midst of the celebration of their ancient festival.

You will have songs as in the night when you keep the festival; and gladness of heart as when one marches to the sound of the flute, to go to the mountain of the Lord, to the Rock of Israel (Isaiah 30:29).

Like those who waited long ago in that upper room for something they had little understanding of, we also wait; we wait for the promise of His coming and our adoption as sons.

Behold, I and the children whom the Lord has given me, are for signs and wonders in Israel from the Lord of Hosts, who dwells on Mount Zion (Isaiah 8:18).

The apostle Paul quotes this Scripture in Hebrews 2:13 when speaking to the believers concerning the believing remnant that will be left on the earth at the end of the age. It will be a day of darkness and distress, a day when the Lord will become a sanctuary to His people. "The people whom I formed for Myself [new creation], will declare My praise" (Is. 43:21). "Everyone who is called by My name, and whom I have created for My glory... (Is. 43:7).

Jesus is getting some people ready for His glory! What does it mean?

> *Ask Me about the things to come concerning My sons...* (Isaiah 45:11b).

God will have sons (Rom. 8:14). Jesus was the firstborn of *many* brethren (Rom. 8:29), a regular company of sons. The Lord speaks of them as *one*, the Body of Christ.

> *"I have aroused him in righteousness, and I will make all his ways smooth; He will build My city, and will let My exiles go free, without any payment or reward," says the Lord of hosts* (Isaiah 45:13).

The world is a mess, but God has a plan and it's moving right along. The glory and restoration are coming. To His chosen He says,

> *...In a favorable time I have answered you, and in a day of salvation I have helped You; and I will keep You and give You for a covenant of the people, to restore the land, to make them inherit the desolate heritages; saying to those who are bound, "Go forth"...* (Isaiah 49:8-9).

My goodness, this is getting interesting, isn't it? On the Day of Pentecost Peter preached, immediately interpreting Old Testament Scriptures and prophecies they were familiar with. He explained that what they had just experienced was the fulfillment of Joel's prophecy (see Acts 2:16-21). No doubt we'll hear some exciting preaching again one of these days as Old Testament Scripture comes alive.

When the exiles returned with Ezra and Nehemiah to rebuild the walls and the temple, the people gathered as *one* to hear Ezra read from the book of the Law of Moses. He read from early morning until midday to those who could understand (see Ezra 8:1-3).

A new day is about to begin for us!

Behold, the former things have come to pass, now I declare new things; before they spring forth I proclaim them to you (Isaiah 42:9).

Jesus inaugurated a new, living way for us to come right into the presence of god. Without fear or guilt, we can come boldly to His throne. He desires very much that we come and "dine" with Him; we can personally fellowship together and He can tell us things we have never known.

He made a way through the veil, that is the flesh. There is no need for a priest between us and the Father. He loves and enjoys His children, and He wants His sons (mature children) to understand the wonderful inheritance He has for them—things too wonderful for us to understand in the natural realm.

Jesus is the only way to the Father; therefore we keep our eyes on Him, the author and finisher of our faith. He is our advocate in Heaven, ready to intercede for us.

There is so much more to this wonderful plan God has worked out for eternity. We sometimes think He moves awfully slow, but He is in no hurry. He operates completely outside of "time."

Chapter 11

Gates of Righteousness

*Open to me the **gates of righteousness**; I shall enter through them, I shall give thanks unto the Lord. This is the gate of the Lord; the righteous will enter through it* (Psalm 118:19-20).

After the Day of Pentecost, the Church Age exploded with power as the gospel of the Kingdom was carried first to the Jew, then to the gentiles through Paul's revelation. It went out into all the "known" world.

The organizational part of the Church also proceeded rapidly, but in the process some things were lost, some were added, and a mixture of some things evolved that weren't there in the beginning. Corruption began to creep into the Church, even before the last apostle died. Outsiders began to come in after Paul. They tried to mix the Law and grace.

With the passing years, the zeal of the original disciples disappeared. It was replaced by dreary orthodoxy, culminating in the Dark Ages, a period barren of any creativity or spiritual growth. With Martin Luther the darkness was penetrated and the restoration of the Church began. He was branded a heretic. He was hated and thrown in jail for his beliefs, but God was on the move when He stirred this man into action, seeing wrongs that needed to be made right.

The curtain was pulled back a little, letting in some light. Eventually the Bible was put into the hands of the people, but none of this happened overnight. There was great opposition. People don't like change, and the things Martin Luther said seemed like sacrilege to them, just as the teachings of Jesus caused Him to be labeled a blasphemer by the scribes and Pharisees. Their constant hounding and questioning of Him might be compared to the type of pressure put on leaders today by reporters and politicians.

There was a long period of time between the early Church and the time of Luther. The darkness settled in heavier and thicker. But God began to move again at closer intervals. Much change and renewal came with the advent of John Wesley, Calvin, and others.

Wesley preached in England, Ireland, and Scotland. Like John the Baptist, Jesus, and Luther, he preached wherever he could, wherever people would gather and listen, even in fields.

The Anglican churches of England wouldn't allow Wesley to preach in their pulpits. He started meetings with groups of twelve people who met once a week for Bible study, prayer, discussion, and encouragement of one another. This was around the year 1742. He trained lay preachers who traveled everywhere. These eventually organized into what later became the Methodist Church. These early denominational churches began with power and the Holy Spirit, and they spread out like a fresh breeze.

God is never static. He is ever on the move, creating, developing, changing, and perfecting. Everything in nature points to this ongoing creative, restorative process. At the end of autumn, a tree drops its leaves; they might cover the apples that have dropped. This process enriches the ground and the seed is encouraged to take root in the mulch. In spring, the blossoms pop out almost overnight. Then after the beauty of the blossom fades, a small apple begins to form. It grows each day in the light of the sun. It may not be very noticeable at first, not until it is nearly mature. Then one day it can be plainly observed. Its change of appearance marks the fact that soon the shiny apple will be ready for eating—the purpose for which it was created.

This is a marvelous parallel to the spiritual picture this example demonstrates concerning God's purpose for Man. The Kingdom of God is not coming with signs to be observed (see Lk. 17:20).

As God's true servants are being groomed by the "husbandman" (Jesus), the precious seed is nurtured and quietly grows toward maturity while hidden away in obscurity, unobserved by others. It will remain inconspicuous, indefinable within the rest of Christendom until the time God chooses for its manifestation. Then there will be a change of appearance, just before the harvest time (like Jesus on the Mount of Transfiguration). This will mark the fact that very soon those who are part of this seed will be involved with the purpose for which they were born.

Truly, truly, I say unto you, unless a grain of wheat fall into the earth and dies, it remains by itself alone; but if it dies, it bears much fruit (John 12:24).

When Jesus spoke these words, He was speaking of His death, burial, and resurrection, and the sending of the Holy Spirit to those who were watching and waiting for the promise. The Body of Christ waits today for His return and for the promise.

As with birth pains, the waves of the Holy Spirit came closer and closer together. From the Day of Pentecost to Martin Luther was a long dark winter. Then two hundred years later there were others like John Wesley when the great denominational churches came into being.

"However, the spiritual is not first, but the natural; then the spiritual" (1 Cor. 15:46). At the turn of this century (during the same time the Zionist movement was birthed) there was a worldwide outpouring of the Holy Ghost. First came the natural "land of Israel," then came the "spiritual Israel," the Church.

That revival created a stir that reverberated around the world. As in the past, this move of God was opposed by the established systems. The people met in homes or empty storefronts. Many established churches didn't believe that the Holy Spirit is for today. Maybe they didn't read the Book of John or Paul's epistles. These "shunned" people eventually became more or less accepted as they became more like the rest of the world, but by then God was moving in a different way.

And I set watchmen over you, saying "Listen to the sound of the trumpet!"... (Jeremiah 6:17).

As is usually the case, some heard the trumpet and got ready for the move. In 1948, forty years after the last great revival, two amazing things happened again. The winds of the Holy Spirit were blowing once more. Foundations were laid at that time for ministries to be used in the mighty ingathering harvest at the end of this age.

While this was happening, the world was stunned when the state of Israel was suddenly born in desolate Palestine after centuries of devastation and barren waste in the land.

Then they will rebuild the ancient ruins, they will raise up the former devastations, and they will repair the ruined cities, the desolations of many generations (Isaiah 61:4).

Yes, the natural comes and then the spiritual. You will remember earlier in this book we learned that the stories about Israel are our examples. They were written down for our instruction, we who are living at the end of the age (1 Cor. 10:11). So at the same time revival was happening in 1948, sure enough, the world's attention was again riveted upon the land of Israel.

Most observers thought the Israelis in the new country would never do much with the wasteland, but they pushed back the sand that had blown in over the years. They drained the mosquito-infested swamps, and they led the world in their experiments with irrigation and other innovative farm techniques.

While setting up their government, they also built a group of musicians into a fine symphony. The world was forced to take note of the Israeli Air Force that boasted of having the finest pilots in the world. The tiny nation was already showing signs of becoming an entity to be reckoned with.

As I recall this, I can't help but think of the coming Kingdom, the thousand-year reign of Christ here on the earth. First comes the natural, then the spiritual. Read on.

Today, this formerly "God-forsaken" land blooms like the garden of Eden (see Is. 51:3). It exudes a vitality and purposefulness that draws young people from all over the world. Their fascination with the people and the land may be a reaction to their own backgrounds, life styles of affluence, or boredom with life. Perhaps they are simply drawn by the energy evoked by those in the land. The land remains an enigma, always drawing the pilgrims and tourists back—back to Jerusalem, back to the haunting beauty of the desert wilderness of the Negev.

The trees in the planted forests have grown tall since my tree was planted there years ago. The trees are changing the weather pattern, so there is now more rainfall. Their Jaffa oranges are shipped all over the world. The restoration project in the "Old City" of Jerusalem has been completed, and it is almost as though Israel is getting ready for a party—the way many people do when they've finished remodeling or redecorating a house.

Israel doesn't realize it, but they are getting ready for their coming King, Yeshua! One of these days the mountain of the Lord will be ascended once more, as God moves on to something *new,* something *big!*

> *Do not call to mind the former things or ponder things of the past. Behold, I will do something new, now it will spring forth; will you not be aware of it?...* (Isaiah 43:18-19).

Abraham ascended the mountain with Isaac, and on the third day when he was ready to offer him as a burnt offering, God spoke to him again, telling him not to do it. A ram was caught in the thicket to serve as a substitute, and the promised covenant was established through Isaac, the child of promise. God had assured Abraham at an earlier time that His covenant could not be established through Ishmael, the son of the bondwoman. Rather, it must be established through the child of the free woman.

At one time God nearly destroyed the Israelites, but Moses interceded for them. While he was on the mountain a second time, he got the instructions for building the Ark of the Covenant and for other holy observances. When he came back down with the tablets written by the hand of God, the people were out of control. They had already forgotten their earlier re-dedication. They no longer feared God. Because their deliverer, Moses, had delayed in coming back down, they made for themselves another god.

Moses had left Aaron the priest in charge, but he became part of the rebellion. Originally, Aaron was to have been Moses' mouthpiece, speaking his words. The restless group talked Aaron into making a god for them. Imagine!

They gave their gold earrings and other things to him, and he melted them down into the form of a golden calf, which became their god. Then Aaron made an altar and they fashioned their own type of religion. It was a mockery of what God had given Moses. They were playing at their counterfeit religion, going through the outward motions of a feast unto the Lord. They had burnt offerings and their own brand of peace offerings.

We can recall how furious Moses was when he came down from the mountain and saw what they had done; he threw down the tablets, shattering them at the foot of the mountain.

And he took the calf which they had made and burned it with fire, and ground it to powder, and scattered it over the surface of the water, and made the sons of Israel drink it (Exodus 32:20).

People today have begun to think that Jesus is never coming back. (Having been conditioned to "instant everything," they hate to wait.) Jesus is no longer real to them. Through the press and entanglement of materialism, they're losing hold of their original faith. Peace and prosperity occupy their minds; the outward form of religion dries up and chokes off any hope held in the past. The noise of Babylon clamors for their attention.

Men no longer fear God. The thing they fear is nuclear pollution! They fear their water supply might become polluted with the powdery residue and they'll have to drink it (see Ex. 32:20).

"Peace, Peace," the monotonous lyrics enlarge, but the melody isn't heard. "Peace, Peace," the media's message clamors; and the people blindly strive after it saying, "Peace, Peace," but there is no peace:

...Everyone is greedy for gain, and from the prophet even to the priest everyone deals falsely. And they have healed the brokenness of My people superficially, saying "Peace, peace," but there is no peace (Jeremiah 6:13-14).

Apart from God there is no peace, and man is beginning to reap the whirlwind resulting from his departure from Almighty God.

When the righteous are in authority, the people rejoice: but when the wicked beareth rule, the people mourn (Proverbs 29:2 KJV).

Man's problems are multiplying so fast he doesn't know which way to turn. When Aaron the priest was left in charge, he got in trouble right along with the others.

"Woe to the shepherds who are destroying and scattering the sheep of My pasture!" declares the Lord (Jeremiah 23:1).

Our lofty humanistic dreams of the past four or five decades are turning into flimsy cobwebs. Our efforts toward peace are progressing outwardly only, while on every corner of the globe people are killing each other and fear grows daily.

"How the faithful city has become a harlot" (Is. 1:21a). She is selling her services in place of a relationship.

We have seen the two cities in the Bible set against each other—Jerusalem, the city of God (the true Church), and Babylon, the harlot city (the apostate church).

A harlot momentarily satisfies the desires of the flesh. The apostle Paul taught that we are to die to the flesh and crucify it; the flesh strives against the spirit (see Gal. 5:17). This act of putting down the flesh was foreshadowed in the Old Testament by the ritual of circumcision, the cutting away of the flesh.

Babylon the harlot reigns over the kings of the earth (see Rev. 17:18). A king has authority over a group of people or a place. We found earlier, in Chapter 8, that it was never God's intention to have earthly kings over His people (see 1 Sam. 8), but His people demanded it.

When nations turn away from God and His guidance, chaos follows with a certainty. "No one sues righteously and no one pleads honestly. They trust in confusion, and speak lies; they conceive mischief, and bring forth iniquity" (Is. 59:4).

Woe to those who call evil good, and good evil...who justify the wicked for a bribe, and take away the rights of the ones who are in the right! (Isaiah 5:20a,23)

In a confused society, the jails will be filled to capacity, houses locked up, and the noise of revelry stopped (see Isaiah 24:7-10).

All joy turns to gloom. The gaiety of the earth is banished. Desolation is left in the city, and the gate is battered to ruins (Isaiah 24:11b-12).

The people have lost their way.

The expression on their faces bears witness against them. And they display their sin like Sodom; they do not even conceal it. Woe to them! For they have brought evil on themselves (Isaiah 3:9).

And I will make mere lads their princes and capricious children will rule over them, and the people will be oppressed, each one by another, and each one by his neighbor; the youth will storm against the elder, and the inferior against the honorable (Isaiah 3:4-5).

"We hope for justice, but there is none..." (Isaiah 59:11b). I didn't copy this from yesterday's newspaper. I copied it all from the Book of Isaiah, from the Bible.

The eyes of God's prophets stretched far into the future, and they could see how we, at the end of this age, would be living. Those who seek for truth can find it faithfully written down by God's servants the prophets.

Surely the Lord God does nothing unless He reveals His secret counsel to His servants the prophets (Amos 3:7).

These prophecies have not been understood until recent times; we draw close to the time for fulfillment.

Our feet are standing within Your gates, O Jerusalem (Psalm 122:2).

*Open to me the **gates of righteousness**; I shall enter through them, I shall give thanks to the Lord. This is the gate of the Lord; the righteous will enter through it* (Psalm 118:19-20).

Listen to me, you who pursue righteousness, who seek the Lord: Look to the rock from which you were hewn, and to the quarry from which you were dug. Look to Abraham your father (Isaiah 51:1-2a).

We did that. We found our bearings, found who we are in Christ. In the Old Testament we saw things that were fulfilled through Christ in the New Testament. We found that Abraham's son, Isaac symbolizes the covenant people, of whom the apostle Paul plainly tells us "we" are. If we are "in Christ," we are Abraham's seed and heirs to the promises of God.

Together we have followed the "roadmarks" in the Old Testament (see Jer. 31:21), which pointed us in the right direction. We are now following hard after righteousness (Jesus, our Melchizidek). We are on the road to Zion, and we are about to *go through the gates*!

Chapter 12

Gates of Zion

What is next on the agenda? What can we expect? Is God's plan still in operation?

Absolutely, God is still in control. Not only is His plan still in effect, but one portion of it is about to climax as this present age comes to its conclusion.

First, the gospel of the Kingdom will be preached throughout all the world for a witness to all nations (see Mt. 24:14). "This is the generation of those who seek Him" (Ps. 24:6a).

On the sixth day God created man, and He was well pleased. We must understand and believe that man is extremely important to God. He has gone to great lengths to ensure man's redemption after Adam's fall.

We've seen the plan moving forward, slowly at first, then gaining momentum in our day. Finally at this time, it is rushing to its climax while humanity holds its breath.

We need to know His ways and understand His plan in order to be sure we are "in the ark." We need to know our proper place within that plan. The apostle Peter gave us an important clue to understanding endtime truths when he said,

But do not let this one fact escape your notice, beloved, that with the Lord one day is as a thousand years, and a thousand years as one day (2 Peter 3:8).

He mentioned this in context with other comments concerning the coming of the Day of the Lord. According to that statement, we are in the sixth day since Adam.

It appears that God's redemptive plan may follow the same pattern as the original creation week. He created man on the sixth day then rested on the seventh, a sabbath.

During the present "sixth day" Jesus has been forming His "New Creation man," who will be conformed to the image of Christ. This is indeed a new thing God is doing.

There was a 2,000 year period between Adam and Abraham, 2,000 years from Abraham to Jesus, and it has been almost 2,000 years now from the life of Jesus to the present time.

The *Day of the Lord* draws near!

If we're coming to the end of the sixth (1,000 year) day, then the seventh would be next, a sabbath rest.

Very soon the "New Man" will be conformed to His image. It will not be of our doing, but Jesus, the author and perfecter of our faith, will see to it. Nothing is too difficult for Him.

Therefore if any man is in Christ, he is a new creature [new breed]; *the old things passed away; behold, new things have come* (2 Corinthians 5:17).

For whom He foreknew, He also predestined to be conformed to the image of His Son, that He might be the first-born among many brethren (Romans 8:29).

The first-born among many brethren? Really?

Yes, this "new man," will be a brother of Jesus. Can you believe it? Jesus said He would not be ashamed to call us brethren (see Heb. 2:11). Even more exciting is the realization that as Jesus' brothers we will be God's adopted sons.

There will be many brothers: "For all who are being led by the Spirit of God, these are the sons of God" (Rom. 8:14). "He predestined us to adoption as sons through Jesus Christ to Himself, according to the kind intention of His will" (Eph. 1:5).

What a heritage! Our Father owns it all, and He wants to share it "because of the kind intention of His will." He just wants to. What a break for us. He wants to give us the desires of our hearts, just as earthly fathers try to do.

The old things have passed away, and new things have come.

The Law served as a tutor under the old covenant, making us aware of our sins; but Jesus came with the new and better covenant. He brought a better solution to sin. With Jesus it's always better and better. Jesus, our pattern, has shown us the new and living way. He passed through the veil of the flesh 2,000 years ago.

*And they commanded the people, saying, "When you see the **ark of the covenant** of the Lord your God with the Levitical priests carrying it, then you shall set out from your place and go after it. However, there shall be between you and it a distance of about 2,000 cubits..."* (Joshua 3:3-4).

Now, 2,000 years later, it's time for us to go after it!

The Maker of the prototypes in Heaven continues with His new creation today. When building the tabernacle, Moses was warned by God to make sure all things are made according to the pattern shown to him on the mountain (see Heb. 8:5). So this new man is being made according to the pattern of Jesus. Jesus fulfills every last thing in the tabernacle of the wilderness.

This new man is the opposite of the first Adam, who was created from the earth and was earthy (see 1 Cor. 15:47). This new man is spiritual, led by the Spirit.

If we carry on with the idea of God's redemption plan being accomplished in six days like His original creation was, we are now at the end of the sixth day, and we are ready to go into the seventh "thousand year" period—the Millennium. Could this be true?

Could this be God's "sabbath rest," a whole thousand years? Could this be the time when they hammer their swords into plowshares and their spears into pruning forks, when they finally quit studying war? (See Isaiah 2:4.) It almost seems too good to be true.

Yes, it looks as though this is the believers' rest spoken of in Hebrews, the one concerning the Israelites from the psalm that Paul referred to: "Therefore I swore in My anger, truly they shall not enter into My rest" (Ps. 95:11). When the apostle Paul explained this to the early Church in Hebrews 4, they were at that time, in a new time frame, a new age. They had moved under the new covenant, into a time when God wanted to move them into something different. The Holy Spirit had been sent!

Jesus had come doing the works of the Father. He accomplished it all; so after His victorious resurrection, when He sent the Holy Spirit it was time for the creation of the "new man." This man, who is formed during the Age of Grace, has a brand new connection to God and Heaven. He has the Holy Spirit living in him, leading him into all truth (see Jn. 16:13). He has a new Teacher, and he is led by the Spirit of God.

The apostle John reminded the believers of how the prophets had written that everyone would be taught of God (see Jn. 6:45). John was trying to tell them that from the early Church in New Testament times until now, the day has arrived when believers can enter the rest that our forefathers failed to enter.

...Yet shall not thy teachers be removed into a corner any more, but thine eyes shall see thy teachers: And thine ears shall hear a word behind thee, saying, This is

the way, walk ye in it, when ye turn to the right hand, and when ye turn to the left (Isaiah 30:20-21 KJV).

There will be teachers (prophets) like Isaiah walking in divine guidance, and the Holy Spirit within us will agree and confirm the teaching. The people of Jerusalem were warned before their destruction. But God poured over them a spirit of deep sleep and shut their "eyes," the prophets, so that the entire vision was to them like the words of a sealed book (see Is. 29:10).

Remembering that the stories about Israel were written as an example for our instruction at the end of this Church Age (see 1 Cor. 10:11), the verses quoted from Isaiah tell us that when we come to this time, the Holy Spirit will guide us from within, the prophets will be restored to the Church, and truth will flow like a river.

And on every lofty mountain and on every high hill there will be streams running with water on the day of the great slaughter, when the towers fall (Isaiah 30:25).

Towers are strong and highly visible. When they fall there is a lot of noise and rubble.

You will have songs as in the night when you keep the festival; and gladness of heart, as when one marches to the sound of the flute, to go to the mountain of the Lord, to the Rock of Israel. And the Lord will cause His voice of authority to be heard... (Isaiah 30:29-30).

His voice of authority will be heard through the mouth of His Body, here on earth (the Holy Spirit-guided Body of Christ). He will be heard through His witnesses (the witness from Heaven and the witness of the Holy Spirit in the Body on earth.) This is the reigning of the Righteous Branch (see Is. 11). "...He will strike the earth with the rod of His mouth... (Is. 11:4). This is the authority of the Word, the Sword of the Spirit. He strikes with the rod, and every blow of the rod is punishment (see Is. 30:31-32).

This "voice of authority" (Is. 30:30) matches the authority granted to the two witnesses (see Rev. 11:3):

And if anyone desires to harm them, fire proceeds out of their mouth and devours their enemies; and if anyone would desire to harm them, in this manner he must be killed (Revelation 11:5).

"For our God is a consuming fire" (Heb. 12:29; see also Deut. 4:24). Here are the "fires of tribulation!"

...His lips are filled with indignation, and His tongue is like a consuming fire (Isaiah 30:27).

Judgment is executed by the authority of the Word of God! David killed the giant, and there was no sword in his hand. He prevailed over the enemy because he came to him "in the name of the Lord of Hosts" (1 Sam. 17:45).

This last revival will have judgment occurring while God displays His glory in the most mighty way ever seen.

You will have songs as in the night when you keep the festival; and gladness of heart as when one marches to the sound of the flute, to go to the mountain of the Lord, to the Rock of Israel (Isaiah 30:29).

Of the three main feasts, the only festival that hasn't been kept is the *Feast of Tabernacles*. When it comes, it will move us into a new realm of the Spirit, this is when God will set His sanctuary in our midst forever (see Ezek. 37:26).

Paul encouraged the Jews in the early Church to press on in their enlightenment and not fall back as their ancestors had done in the wilderness. He didn't want them going back to the Law just because that was what they'd known all their lives. The Law was of "works," and it was being made obsolete (see Heb. 10:9). "He takes away the first in order to establish the second" (Heb. 10:9b).

...I will put My Laws into their minds, and I will write them upon their hearts. And I will be their God, and they shall be My people. And they shall not teach everyone his fellow citizen, and everyone his brother, saying, "Know the Lord," for all shall know Me, from the least to the greatest of them (Hebrews 8:10-11).

"...For the earth will be full of the knowledge of the Lord as the waters cover the sea" (Is. 11:9; see also Hab. 2:14).

Some teach that there will never be another great revival, that the world will just get worse and worse, but certainly these Scriptures refute this. This festival *will* be kept, just as surely as the other two were. The Festival of Ingathering (*Feast of Tabernacles*) will be fulfilled. It will be a feast of great joy!

The new covenant was meant to bring us toward maturity under the guidance of the Holy Spirit following Pentecost. Except that some, having begun by the Spirit, tried to be perfected by the flesh through going back to the Law (Gal. 3:3). Paul admonished the "foolish" Galatians for this (see Gal. 3:1). He also scolded the Hebrew believers:

For though by this time you ought to be teachers, you have need again for someone to teach you the elementary principle of the oracles of God, and you have come to need milk and not solid food (Hebrews 5:12).

Solid food is for the mature. These words are not just for those in the early Church; the members of the Church of our time have stayed on milk far too long, playing around like babes (see Heb. 5:13-14). Judgment is coming, and judgment begins at the house of the Lord.

At the end of the age in which Noah lived, judgment came in the form of a great flood. Noah and his family were prepared; they were in the ark. We must keep in mind that Jesus is our *Ark*.

As the water increased, Noah's ark was "lifted up above the earth" and it "rested" on the mountains on the seventeenth day of the seventh month (see Gen. 8:4). I love the symbolism here! Think about it a moment.

So what does this have to do with us today?

The *Feast of Tabernacles* would be in progress on the seventeenth day of the seventh month. Could this date be just a coincidence? I don't think so. No wonder Peter got so excited on the Mount of Transfiguration, wanting to build booths as they'd done each year since the wilderness experience to celebrate the festival.

Paul saw that they hadn't entered the rest in his day, and it's pretty plain that we haven't today. Clearly for the most part, we are still laboring in the flesh concerned with outward form and works.

Paul said he was running the race with patience. He was looking forward to the time when we might all "...attain to the unity of the faith, and of the knowledge of the Son of God, to a mature man, to the measure of the stature which belongs to the fulness of Christ" (Eph. 4:13).

Maturity is of extreme importance. Kids are cute, but the Church needs to grow up. David, though anointed as a child, didn't reign until manhood. Likewise Jesus' ministry didn't begin until he was of full age, in the fullness of time.

By wondering how we come to this maturity, we find Paul explaining in Hebrews that even the giants of faith did not receive the promise because "God had provided something better for us, so that apart from us, they should not be made perfect (complete) even though they had gained approval through their faith" (see Heb. 11:39). They had to wait for us, for the end of the age. Remember, this is something *big* that God has planned, something *new*!

> *...Forgetting those things which are behind, and reaching forth unto those things which are before, I press toward the mark of for the prize of the high calling of God in Christ Jesus* (Philippians 3:13-14 KJV).

The high calling of sonship through adoption (Rom. 8:23)—that's what Paul was after. A mature son can be a great help to his father in his business. Jesus said, "I must work the works of Him that sent me" (Jn. 9:4 KJV). A son is quite different than a hireling to a father.

Taking Paul's advice would help us attain this. We must forget what was behind, no matter how much we enjoy reviewing our past accomplishments. Our goal is to keep our eyes on Jesus. We need to be moving on wherever He takes us; we want to be sealed with the mind of Christ.

The Body of Christ here on earth will have one "Head" (mind). Impossible though it may seem, through the *Living Word* and the power of the Holy Spirit, we are being conformed to His image. Jesus prayed His high priestly prayer with that in mind.

> *That they may all be one; even as Thou, Father, art in Me, and I in Thee, that they also may be in Us; that the world may believe that Thou didst send Me* (John 17:21).

When Jesus prayed "that they may all be one," He wasn't talking about some ecumenical man-made unity. He was referring to the unity He has with the Father.

> *...That you may know and understand that the Father is in Me, and I in the Father* (John 10:38).

"...Christ in you, the hope of glory" (Col. 1:27): That was the mystery that was hidden from past generations but was manifested to His saints in the New Testament. When the Body of Christ is joined to its Head (Jesus Christ), the world will know because we will be one.

So we wait for the promise. We don't know all the details, but we wait, just as the hundred and twenty in the upper room waited for the promise of the Holy Ghost (the new thing that was about to happen). They gathered as one and waited during the *Feast of Pentecost*.

When will the promise come to us? When will we enter the rest of God?

It would be a pretty good guess to say, "when the Jews are celebrating the *Feast of Tabernacles*"; the promise of the Holy Ghost was fulfilled while the Jews were celebrating *Feast of Pentecost*, just as Passover was fulfilled while the Jews celebrated the *Feast of Passover*.

Some things are certain. It will be when we come "to the measure of the stature which belongs to the fulness of Christ" (Eph. 4:13b); when we are "transformed by the renewing of [our] mind[s]" (Rom. 12:2); when "the morning star arises in [our] hearts" (2 Pet. 1:19); and when Zion is built up (Ps. 102:16).

O.K. What is Zion? What do we know about it?

Zion was the highest elevation in Jerusalem. That was where David's throne was and where the ark was after David brought it home. David's warriors were at Zion. In his maturity David began to reign there, and the Law went forth from Zion.

Today, while waiting for the promise of His coming and the manifestation of the promise, we are once again reminding one another to steady our eyes on Jesus, the author and finisher of our faith. (I'm so glad He is doing it and that it's not up to me.) The Lord is the builder. He didn't care for the building going on at Babel.

God's house will not be slapped together with the flammable substance from the earth, like the pitch used in the building of Noah's ark, Moses' basket, and the brick cities in the plains of Shinar. Abraham had no interest in these cities. They were built fast, and they all looked alike, in total opposition to God's creation; each animal, plant, and tiny flower has its own distinct character.

One can see why God didn't care for that type of building. The *house of God* (the temple), will be built with individual "living" stones. Each is unique and beautiful, comfortably fitted together with the others. In God's Kingdom there is neither Greek nor Jew, Black nor White (see Rom. 10:12; Gal. 3:28).

No, this house will have to stand through the fire of God's presence. Our ark needs nothing to hold it together. This house of God that Jacob saw in the vision of the ladder somehow connected Heaven and earth. Indeed, might this be part of the glorious freedom of the children of God (see Rom. 8:21)?

...Things which eye has not seen and ear has not heard, and which have not entered into the heart of man all that God has prepared for those who love Him (1 Corinthians 2:9).

Noah's ark had three decks, just as the tabernacle in the wilderness had three compartments. There were three main Jewish feasts unto the Lord, and Jesus said there would be a thirtyfold, sixtyfold, and a hundredfold increase with the seed sown (see Mt. 13:18). We know there is a third heaven (2 Cor. 12:2), so there must be a first and second as well.

The builder is building, but we don't see anything except a confusing mess at this point, like the boards and scaffolding. Jesus said He would prepare a place for us, so that we could be where He is (Jn. 14:2). He also mentioned many dwelling places in His House. At this time we don't know upon which deck we'll find ourselves, in what compartment or fold, but we wait for the promise of His coming.

Times and epochs are in the Father's hands. "But when the fullness of the time came, God sent forth His Son, born of a woman..." (see Gal. 4:4).

We are the temple of God (see 1 Cor. 3:16), a temple not made with hands (see Mt. 14:58). We are Christ's house (Heb. 3:6)!

When the Lord has built up Zion and appeared in His glory, He will regard the prayer of the destitute and not despise their prayer. This is written for the generation to come that a people yet to be created may praise the Lord. (See Psalms 102:16-18.)

David was prophesying future things in this psalm—the new creation, things in the latter days, and a time of climax.

So then this perfect Church "without spot or wrinkle" (Eph. 5:20) doesn't necessarily have a steeple?

Right! This is the Kingdom of God on earth. It is a Kingdom of priests and kings—the "called-out" nation, chosen of God. That's what we're talking about. It's the same Kingdom that God had in mind back in Abraham's time, as well as when He commissioned Moses to deliver His people from the bondage of Egypt. He sought to form them into a holy nation. (You can't *join* this nation.)

The United States of America was once "one nation under God"; it is so stated in our Pledge of Allegiance. We were once known as a Christian nation, but now we have a different pharaoh, one who doesn't know Joseph (Jesus). Once again we find ourselves oppressed in the same place of earlier blessings, just as in the story of Joseph and the Children of Israel.

We have been talking about the "covenant people," who are symbolized by Isaac the seed of Abraham. We all know that all who are in Christ are Abraham's seed and heirs according to the promise. (There again is that inheritance, the birthright that Esau so carelessly threw away.)

This is the New Testament reenactment of the symbolic story of Joseph and his brothers. God's marvelous giant computer not only keeps track of what's happening now and what happened through the centuries, but it keeps track of what is going to happen in the future.

Joseph was chosen of God. His father favored him and gave him a bright priestly coat of many colors. His jealous brothers tried to do away with him. However, it turned out later that he was at the right place at the right time to be a blessing to his brethren who were so in need during the famine.

> *"Behold, days are coming," declares the Lord God, "When I will send a famine on the land, not a famine for bread or a thirst for water, but rather for hearing the words of the Lord"* (Amos 8:11).

Joseph's barns are full, ready for the need; this story is repeated in these last days. Instead of Israel of old, this time it is spiritual Israel, the Church, that is hungry for the grain.

Israel and the Church were one body at the beginning of the Church Age. The early Church was Jewish until Acts 10. Later, Paul was sent to the heathen gentiles. It was a shocking idea at first. The nations around Israel were all pagan, thus the words *nation, gentile,* and *heathen* were all interchangeable. The Jews were God's own people.

Now, after Israel is restored as a nation at the end of this age, the two peoples will again become one olive tree. We have been taught that this will happen during the last seven years of Daniel's weeks of years. (See Daniel 9:20-27.)

> *The Lord loves the **gates of Zion** more than all the dwelling places of Jacob. Glorious things are spoken of you, O city of God* (Psalm 87:2-3).

It sounds like the *gates of Zion* might be a good place to dwell, kind of like living on Nob Hill (the wealthy part of town). If God loves Zion more than any other place, that's where I want to be. When Jesus told His disciples He was going away to prepare a place for them, He promised to come again and receive them unto Himself, that they might be where He is.

Back in Chapter 5 we saw that Joseph paved the way; he was at the right place in the time of need, during the famine. He was in a place of influence so that he could bring his brethren to where He was—at the palace. They were given some of the best land in Egypt because of who he was and because of their relationship with him.

Indeed, Joseph is a clear "type" of Jesus; He wants to bring His brothers (us) to where He is. The Father knows the time.

...I will appoint you as a covenant to the people, as a light to the nations, to open blind eyes, to bring out the prisoners from the dungeon, and those who dwell in darkness from the prison (Isaiah 42:6-7).

The Lord longs to speak to His people. He first tells the prophets.

...In the last days, the mountain of the house of the Lord will be established as the chief of the mountains [kingdoms], *and will be raised up above the hills; and all nations will stream to it* (Isaiah 2:2; see also Micah 4:1).

For the Lord of hosts will have a day of reckoning against everyone...who is lifted up, that he may be abased (Isaiah 2:12).

And the daughter of Zion is left like a shelter in a vineyard, like a watchman's hut in a cucumber field, like a besieged city (Isaiah 1:8).

Come down and sit in the dust, O virgin daughter of Babylon; sit on the ground without a throne... (Isaiah 47:1).

It looks like things will be switched around a bit. The daughter of Zion has about had it, and the daughter of Babylon is being dethroned. It sounds like it might be judgment day. Things definitely are being shaken, but whatever is of God will remain standing.

We've talked about the two cities in the Bible that are set against each other—Jerusalem and Babylon. Now we have two women mentioned, the daughter of Zion and the daughter of Babylon. One has surely been through the storms. She has been waiting out of the mainstream, apart from the others. She has been just trying to hold on a little longer, watching and remaining alert to the enemy. The other, the daughter of Babylon, is mockingly invited to come down and sit in the dust for a change as she is removed from her throne. She seems to be the mystery harlot of Revelation 17. She is about to be judged while the other daughter is about to receive the former dominion.

And as for you, tower of the flock, hill of the daughter of Zion, to you it will come—even the former dominion will come, the kingdom of the daughter of Jerusalem (Micah 4:8).

Who is this daughter of Zion? What is this former dominion?

Do you remember that Jesus said He came to "seek and to save that which was lost" (Lk. 19:10)? When

Adam fell from grace in the garden, satan stole not only man's eternal life but also the dominion God had given him.

We will leave the daughter of Zion (the inhabitant of Jerusalem) there like a besieged city, for now. We have pretty well traced the restoration of Israel as a nation right along with the restoration of the true Church, and we can see the clear parallel.

There is a time period that we don't like to think about. It is called the *"time of Jacob's trouble"* (see Jer. 30:7 KJV). The traditional teaching is that God deals with the Jews during this time, but I suspect there is something we've missed here. Jacob, whose name means "supplanter," wrestled all through the night with the angel of the Lord, and when the night was over, God changed his name to "Israel." To *supplant*, of course, is to supersede or do something "in place of."

The dark night of the tribulation will be long, and the parallel fits; Jacob in the natural (the land of Israel) will surely have trouble through the dark confusing night. When his strength is gone and he's out of ideas, when the enemy surrounds the state of Israel, God Himself will step in and fight for Israel. As the long night comes to an end, the natural Jacob will see his mistake. He will submit in the face of God and recognize his Messiah just as the dawn is breaking. He will receive the blessing; his name will be changed to Israel, and he will then move to Bethel (the house of God). (See Genesis 35:1.) This is the Jewish remnant.

But he is a Jew who is one inwardly; and circumcision is that which is of the heart, by the Spirit, not by the letter; and his praise is not from men, but from God (Romans 2:29).

I fear that Jacob, in the spiritual sense as well as the natural land of Israel, shall be caught off guard when night falls and man's work is done. (Old hymnals once had a song about this.) It is so difficult to see clearly in darkness, and it is easy to be deceived in the confusion of the shadowy figures and lack of light. Perhaps you've already noticed people getting quite confused over things that should be simple—like what is right and what is wrong. Everything is getting grey and blurred. They call "evil good and good evil" (Is. 5:20).

For behold, darkness shall cover the earth, and deep darkness the peoples (Isaiah 60:2a).

In the apostle John's vision, he was instructed not to measure the court that was outside because it would be given to the nations (heathen) to be trampled for three and a half years. The picture formed here is that a part of the Church, perhaps that part that believes in God, attends church, but has experienced an extended famine (for the Word) right here in Canaan (so to speak) may have been lulled into sleep by endless unchallenging talk of "Peace, Peace" (see Jer. 6:14).

In her peaceful slumber—or stupor—she (the woman or church) may not have even noticed when "uncircumcised foreigners" (see Ezek. 44:7) infiltrated the church. In the book of Esther, Haman (satan) was in the outer court when Esther finally put on her royal robes (Esther 6:4).

> *...They stagger, but not from strong drink. For the Lord has poured over you a spirit of deep sleep, He has shut your eyes, the prophets; and He has covered your heads, the seers. And the entire vision shall be to you like a sealed book* (Isaiah 29:9-11a).

> *Then the Lord said, "Because this people draw near with their words and honor Me with their lip service, but they remove their hearts far from Me, and their reverence for Me consists of tradition learned by rote, therefore behold, I will once again deal marvelously with this people, wondrously marvelous; and the wisdom of their wise men shall perish and the discernment of their discerning men shall be concealed"* (Isaiah 29:13-14).

No, I'm afraid it isn't just the men of Judah (the Jews) who are blind or whose vision is blurred. There are others who reverence God with tradition learned by rote (routine or repetition).

We are living in a time of transition, and that kind of day is not comfortable. When the present shaking is finished, only those things which are of God will stand, the things which have foundations (see Heb. 12:27).

> *For thus says the Lord of hosts, "Once more in a little while, I am going to shake the heavens and the earth, the sea also and the dry land. And I will shake all the nations; and I will fill this house with glory," says the Lord of hosts* (Haggai 2:6).

The house of God will be filled with glory! This is the fulfillment of Jacob's ladder, the gate of Heaven.

In this book, through our quest for truth, we have looked back to the "rock from which we were hewn," just as God suggested to me while I was at the wall in Jerusalem years ago. As instructed, we have looked to Abraham, and to the quarry from which we were dug (see Is. 51:1).

From this point of reference we have determinedly started up the road to Zion, carefully noting the roadmarks along the way, that we might arrive at that city that has foundations, the same city Abraham went looking for, the one glorious city of God (see Jer. 31:21).

How long, O Lord, will I call for help, and Thou wilt not hear?...Strife exists and contention arises. Therefore, the law is ignored and justice is never upheld. For the wicked surround the righteous; therefore, justice comes out perverted (Habakkuk 1:2-4).

How long will we cry? Does God hear us?

...The vision is yet for the appointed time; it hastens toward the goal, and it will not fail. Though it tarries, wait for it; for it will certainly come, it will not delay (Habakkuk 2:3).

We have tried to learn God's ways, and we pray for revelation knowledge, but at best we are seeing through a mirror dimly (see 1 Cor. 13:12). In speaking of the restoration of the natural Jews, the apostle Paul was careful to explain that it isn't because they deserve it (just as we don't), "but from the standpoint of God's choice they are beloved for the sake of the fathers" (Rom.

11:28b). God doesn't forget His covenants. The gifts and callings of God are irrevocable (Rom. 11:29).

So we wait for the vision though it tarries: "For yet in a very little while, He who is coming will come, and will not delay" (Heb. 10:37).

Therefore, do not throw away your confidence, which has a great reward (Hebrews 10:35).

Know this first of all, that in the last days mockers will come with their mocking, following after their own lusts and sayings "where is the promise of His coming? For ever since the fathers fell asleep, all continues just as it was from the beginning of creation" (2 Peter 3:3-4).

The mockers are with us today. They have been here all along. Some are simply rebels toward God; others have been disillusioned by man's religious systems and hypocrisy. Families that once looked for His coming, who kept His commandments and lived with the hope, are now derelict as the storm approaches. They have drifted away from the sheepfolds.

Somewhere along the way, the powerful message of hope became garbled and ungainly as it was replaced with the tendency toward secular exposition, which is humanistic interpretation of spiritually appraised truths (see 1 Cor. 2:14); devoid of Holy Ghost anointing, irrelevant to man's deepest needs, confusion remains and truth stays obscured.

Therefore My people go into exile for their lack of knowledge; and their honorable men are famished, and their multitude is parched with thirst (Isaiah 5:13).

Saul's policy of withholding food has devastated his house. Like Jonathan, these people are still committed to Saul. Not wanting to seem disloyal, they hunger while listening to his voice. "My people are destroyed for lack of knowledge..." (Hos. 4:6).

> *"Woe to the shepherds who are destroying and scattering the sheep of My pasture!" declares the Lord. ... "Behold, the days are coming," declares the Lord, "when I shall raise up for David a righteous Branch; and He will reign as king and act wisely and do justice and righteousness in the land. In his days Judah will be saved and Israel will dwell securely"* (Jeremiah 23:1,5-6a).

True Jews are from the tribe of Judah, and *Israel* is the name God gave Jacob after he wrestled with the angel of the Lord all night long. Both Jeremiah and Isaiah wrote about the righteous branch that suddenly appears at a time of spiritual famine and unrest.

"Then a shoot will spring from the stem of Jesse, and a branch from his roots will bear fruit" (Is. 11:1). This branch will have the spirit of wisdom and understanding, and he will strike the earth with the rod of his mouth (the rod of iron rule, the power of the Word).

This isn't too hard to figure out. Jesse was David's father, and the scribes said that the Christ was the son of David. We know that David represents God's warrior saints, and that David is a type of Christ. Jesus said He was the true vine and we the branches (see Jn. 15:1).

This branch from the stem of Jesse will bear much fruit, because the branches are "in Christ," in the ark ("I in Him and He in Me") and conformed to His image.

We have thrown around a lot of names, names of groups, women, cities, etc., which seem to have much in common. They all seem destined for some climactic event in the near future. The stories from the Old Testament intertwine and come to the same point. Like spokes in a wheel, they all come together at the hub. The Lord wants very much to speak to His people. He wants them to know His ways and be aware of His long-range plan, which is about to reach its crescendo point.

It's all there; God has it cleverly hidden within those Old Testament stories in the Scriptures. He is a rewarder of those who diligently seek Him (see Heb. 11:6).

He gives hidden revelation to those who dine with Him, just as He did with His original disciples. He taught the multitudes in parables, but He took His disciples apart from the others and "explained" them saying.

...To you it has been granted to know the mysteries of the kingdom of heaven, but to them [the multitudes] *it has not been granted* (Matthew 13:11).

Of the others (the multitudes), he said,

...You will keep on hearing, but will not understand; and you will keep on seeing, but will not perceive; for the heart of this people has become dull (Matthew 13:14-15a).

Only those who love and seek Him, who take time with Him, will have understanding of the hidden truths. So we study these various cities, people, groups, etc., and a much larger picture begins to emerge, especially for those who have a renewed mind that is "fine-tuned" to the Word of God.

We have barely touched on the woman who births the manchild, in Revelation 12. She appears to represent the true, visible, or recognized Church at the end of the age. She is in labor to give birth to the child that has been growing and maturing in her womb (or body); the child has been hidden from the world—alive but obscured. "For the Lord has created a new thing in the earth—a woman will encompass a man" (Jer. 31:22b).

This woman has to go to the wilderness as soon as the baby is born, apparently because of the birth and the persecution accompanying the fact. God has a place prepared for her, a place where she will be nourished and protected.

The people and groups we have been discussing definitely seem to be God's chosen—His sons, of whom Jesus was the first, led by the Spirit and about to come to the adoption (like Jewish boys who reach the age of accountability and celebrate their Bar Mitzvah).

This is the manchild, God's army, David's warriors, the overcoming saints, to whom God gave these seven wonderful promises. They will:

1. Eat of the Tree of Life (Rev. 2:7).
2. Not be hurt by the second death (Rev. 2:11).
3. Be given hidden manna and a new name (Rev. 2:17).
4. Be given authority over the nations (Rev. 2:26).

5. Be clothed in white (Rev. 3:5).
6. Be made a pillar in the temple of God (Rev. 3:12).
7. Sit with Jesus on His throne (Rev. 3:21).

Now it will come about that in the last days, the mountain of the house of the Lord will be established as the chief of the mountains, and will be raised above the hills; and all the nations will stream to it. And many peoples will come and say, "Come, let us go up to the mountain of the Lord, to the house of the God of Jacob; that He may teach us, concerning His ways, and that we may walk in His paths." For the law will go forth from Zion, and the word of Lord from Jerusalem. And He will judge between the nations, and render decisions for many peoples; and they will hammer their swords into plowshares, and their spears into pruning hooks. Nation will not lift up sword against nation, and never again will they learn war (Isaiah 2:2-4, see also Micah 4:1).

The above Scriptures, set down verbatim, give a pretty clear picture of what we have been leading up to with all of the preceding foundational setting, the triumphant continuing victory of the finished work of Jesus Christ, the glory of the Church without spot or wrinkle (see Eph. 5:26-27).

Are we not in the last days? Have we seen this in the past? Then we can surely look forward to His coming and the establishment of His Kingdom. Actually, it was established at His first coming, but it will be set in motion at His second coming. It will happen at the first resurrection when the dead in Christ rise first and those of us who are alive and remain shall be "caught up together with them, in the clouds to meet the Lord in the air" (1 Thess. 4:16-17). And thus we shall always be with the Lord. In resurrection bodies we will return to earth with the Lord when He comes in power and great glory. He will come with the armies of heaven following Him, clothed in white linen and riding white horses.

This is what many refer to as the Rapture of the Church. "The armies of heaven" apparently means the army of resurrected saints already in heaven, and the army from the earth who rose to join them in the air in their new resurrection bodies to return with them to the earth.

Blessed and holy is the one who has part in the first resurrection; over these the second death has no power, but they will be priests of God and of Christ and will reign with Him for a thousand years (Revelation 20:6).

We just got ahead of ourselves, but I wanted to sneak in a little preview of the coming glory and victory with Christ.

Now, things are coming along. We see that satan will be bound for a thousand years, and people will quit studying war; they will be delighted to go with their friends to the mountain of the Lord to learn His ways.

Earlier in this chapter, we talked about the fire of God's presence, and His tongue being like a consuming fire—the fire and authority of the Word of God. When Jesus comes with His armies,

...From His mouth comes a sharp sword, so that with it He may smite the nations; and He will rule them with a rod of iron... (Revelation 19:15).

The salvation, the power, and the kingdom of our God and the authority of His Christ will come (see Rev. 12:10).

We aren't quite there yet, so we encourage one another as we wait.

I believe that when these pilgrimages begin, when people quit warring and desire to learn God's ways, when God has poured out His Spirit on all flesh (Joel 2:28), people will call their friends to go along, and it will be very festive. People will arrange vacations for it. I picture them in fine hotels. There will be great joy in meeting old friends, just as it was with us when we got the call from our daughter saying, "Let's go to Jerusalem." Once there, we experienced a new type of worship experience from coming together with thousands of people from all over the world, all with the same vision of the Kingdom. The music and pageantry was, I imagine, only a hint of what the Lord has in store for us in the very near future.

Judgment is coming and so is glory. We know we'll be safe in the Ark as God's indignation passes.

Come, my people, enter into your rooms, and close your doors behind you; hide for a little while, until indignation runs its course. For behold, the Lord is about to come out from His place to punish the inhabitants of the earth for their iniquity (Isaiah 26:20-21a).

> *For in the day of trouble He will conceal me in His tabernacle; in the secret place of His tent He will hide me. He will lift me up on a rock* (Psalm 27:5).

> *He will dwell on the heights; his refuge will be the impregnable rock; his bread will be given him; his water will be sure* (Isaiah 33:16).

Those on Mount Zion, the ones who follow the lamb wherever He goes will have entered God's rest; they will be finished with works and warfare. They will be in the presence of God before His throne. The mountain of the Lord will have been ascended once more, and a new day will have begun.

> *And He will lift up a standard for the nations, and will assemble the banished ones of Israel, and will gather the dispersed of Judah from the four corners of the earth* (Isaiah 11:12).

At that time, ready or not, God's plan will shift into an exciting, higher realm. God's attention will once again be focused on Judah and the banished ones of Israel who will be gathered together, finally, after their long and lonely exile.

Ezekiel's dry bones will have breath enter them, and the body he saw will come to life and live again as the awaited promise comes to fulfillment (see Ezek. 37:5). (It is interesting to check out these words in the Greek and Hebrew: *breath, wind, Spirit,* and *air*; they can almost be used interchangeably.) When the *breath* enters the bones seen by Ezekiel, Judah and Israel will be joined by God to be one nation in the land on the mountains of Israel.

A new government will be established, a government of which there shall be no end of its increase (Is. 9:7).

This is not the government that many are hoping to establish as the new age begins. although elaborate network plans have been laid, this counterfeit kingdom that is anticipated by some will come to nothing when the *real* Messiah King comes to establish His Kingdom. Jesus alone is worthy.

Then it will come about in that day that the nations will resort to the root of Jesse, who will stand as a signal for the peoples; and His resting place will be glorious (Isaiah 11:10).

...And they will all have one shepherd; and they will walk in My ordinances, and keep My statutes, and observe them...and I will make a covenant of peace with them; it will be an everlasting covenant with them and [I] *will set My sanctuary in their midst forever* (Ezekiel 37:24,26).

It sounds like a return to paradise. It will be as in the time of Adam and Eve when God walked and talked with them in the garden. What about Heaven coming to earth? Heaven is where God's throne is, but God won't dwell where sin reigns. He withdrew His presence after Adam's fall.

Remember that Abraham was standing in the presence of God during the destruction of Sodom and was untouched by it. Remember also, that when judgment came in the form of a flood during Noah's time, "...the water increased and lifted up the ark, so that it rose above the earth" (Gen. 7:17). What fantastic symbolism! "And in the seventh month, on the seventeenth day of the month, the ark *rested* upon the mountains of Ararat" (Gen. 8:4).

And I will make all My mountains a road, and My highways will be raised up (Isaiah 49:11).

Go through, go through the gates; clear the way for the people; build up, build up the highway... (Isaiah 62:10).

And a highway will be there, a roadway, and it will be called, the Highway of Holiness (Isaiah 35:8).

...The people who survived the sword found grace in the wilderness—Israel, when it went to find its rest (Jeremiah 31:2).

The "sword of the Lord" is brought out, never to return to its sheath (see Ezek. 21:5). The sword of the spirit, which is the word of God, becomes the weapon of choice in John's revelation (Rev. 1:16).

From Jesus' mouth comes a sharp, two-edged sword. His Body, the Body of Christ here on earth, is fighting a strange battle. They walk, and God does the fighting.

With the "rod of His mouth" this righteous branch will strike the earth, and with the *breath* of His lips, He will slay the wicked (Is. 11:14). His lips are filled with indignation, and His tongue is like a consuming fire (Is. 30:27). The people who survive the sword will find grace in the wilderness (Jer. 31:2). Judgment seems to be connected with that sword, perhaps the peoples' reactions to the Word of God becomes their judgment. Nevertheless, at the same time, much grace will abound in the wilderness.

And on every lofty mountain and on every high hill there will be streams running with water on the day of the great slaughter, when the towers fall (Isaiah 30:25).

With weeping they shall come, and by supplication I will lead them; I will make them walk by streams of waters... (Jeremiah 31:9).

"In those days and at that time," declares the Lord, "the sons of Israel will come, both they and the sons of Judah as well; they will go along weeping as they go, and it will be the Lord their God they will seek. They will ask the way to Zion, turning their faces in its direction; they will come that they may join themselves to the Lord in an everlasting covenant that will not be forgotten (Jeremiah 50:4-5).

This forms a pretty clear picture of a time of judgment and grace; at the same time it will be a time of deep darkness and glory, depending upon which side you belong to and your standing with God.

My dwelling place also will be with them; and I will be their God, and they will be My people. And the nations will know that I am the Lord who sanctifies Israel, when My sanctuary is in their midst forever (Ezekiel 37:27-28).

Looking up the word *sanctuary* in the Hebrew, it is defined as a consecrated thing or place pronounced "clean," a holy place. The *America Heritage Dictionary* provides these definitions: "the most holy part of a sacred place; a place that provides refuge" and "a place that provides refuge, asylum, or immunity from arrest." (Unbelievers will then know that God has set His people apart for special blessings.)

For in the day of trouble He will conceal me in His tabernacle; in the secret place of His tent He will hide me... (Psalm 27:5).

"But this is the covenant which I will make with the house of Israel after those days," declares the Lord, "I will put My Laws within them, and on their heart I will write it; and I will be their God, and they shall be My people" (Jeremiah 31:33).

And they shall not teach everyone his fellow citizen, and everyone his brother, saying, "Know the Lord," for all shall know Me, from the least to the greatest of them (Hebrews 8:11, see also Jeremiah 31:34).

Listen! Your watchmen lift up their voices, they shout joyfully together; for they will see with their own eyes when the Lord restores Zion (Isaiah 52:8)

Before she travailed, she brought forth; before her pain came, she gave birth to a boy. Who has ever heard such a thing? Who has seen such things? Can a land be born in a day? Can a nation be brought forth all at once? As soon as Zion travailed, she also brought forth her sons (Isaiah 66:7-8).

Soon God will have His holy nation!

Although there is a famine in the land (for the Word of God), Joseph has stored the grain, and the woman will be nourished in the wilderness. Her place is prepared, and she will be safe there from the dragon for three and a half years.

Standing before the woman, the dragon (satan), waited to devour the baby when it was born. He was enraged when he saw that the manchild who was to rule the nations with a rod of iron was caught up to God and His throne where he could not touch him (see Rev. 12).

If this truly is a replay, as we might assume, then she will have to flee from her rightful place to the wilderness where she will find grace:

Go through, go through the gates; clear the way for the people; build up, build up the highway; remove the stones, lift up a standard over the peoples. Behold, the Lord has proclaimed to the end of the earth, say to the daughter of Zion, "Lo, your salvation comes; behold His reward is with Him and His recompense before Him," and they will call them, "The holy people, the redeemed of the Lord"; and you will be called, "sought out, a city not forsaken" (Isaiah 62:10-12).

Then they will rebuild the ancient ruins, they will raise up the former devastations, and they will repair the ruined cities, the desolations of many generations (Isaiah 61:4).

God's house will be put back in order. Jacob will now be teachable. He will no longer be called "supplanter." His name will be changed to "Israel," and he will move to Bethel (house of God).

The prophets never did "see" the Church as we know it. Isaiah, in trying to describe what he saw, wrote in terms relating to his day. The nations around Israel were called "gentiles," and God's people were called "Jews." This word is a shortened nickname for "Judah." In Abraham's time they were not considered *Jews*, but *Hebrews*. Only after the twelve tribes were formed were there *Jews* (from the tribe of Judah). So in recording his vision Isaiah spoke of Israel and Judah, the divided kingdom. The other nations around them were referred to as gentiles, nations, or heathen. Today, we would call them unbelievers.

The importance of the Book of Isaiah is indicated by the fact that it is quoted so many times in the New Testament. Even Jesus in the temple read from the scroll of Isaiah, saying, "Today this Scripture has been fulfilled in your hearing" (Lk. 4:21).

As was mentioned earlier, God's holy nation Israel began as one nation; then later it split and became two. The northern territory was called Israel, and it was composed of the ten tribes, each with its own banner and identity.

The southern Kingdom was called Judah. It was composed of two tribes, Judah and Benjamin (and the

Levites). Some of the Levites from the northern kingdom sought asylum in Judah, but some were part of the rebellion in Israel.)

So we have Isaiah in the Old Testament trying to describe a divine vision in words from his own setting, a vision that concerns God's people today at the end of the age.

God's holy nation in the New Testament (the Church) started out as *one,* just like Israel began as one nation but then became divided.

As we wait for the consummation or climax of this portion of God's plan, in our weariness and frustration we often feel like saying, "Lord, can't you hurry"; but rest assured, it will come. He will come and not a minute late.

When the Pharisees questioned Jesus about the Kingdom, He said, "The kingdom of God is not coming with signs to be observed" (Lk. 17:20). This is like the dawn; when it seems the very darkest, suddenly dawn is here and there's light!

Jesus told His disciples that the end of the age would be just as in the days of Noah and Lot. (The people would be doing what they always do, totally unaware, until suddenly the flood of judgment comes.) In both cases, Noah and Lot, the wicked were swept away and the righteous stayed. There will be two people in a bed; one will be taken and one left (see Lk. 17:20-37). In the case of Lot, while he may not have been chosen, he went along with Abraham. Not really understanding the calling, he caused Abraham a lot of trouble. Just before the destruction of Sodom, the angels literally had to go and "take Lot by the hand" to get him to safety outside the city. God remembered him because of his relationship with Abraham; he was part of the household.

Isaiah, Jeremiah, and the minor prophets who are quoted frequently throughout the last part of this book, lived more than two thousand years ago. Try to keep this in mind. See if you can picture Isaiah struggling to find words to describe a vision that would be fulfilled now at the end of this age.

Even a hundred years ago we didn't have cars, let alone airplanes. Isaiah might have called them horses and birds with wheels, etc. Do you see what this may mean?

I'm not going to spell it out, but even the word *tribes*, whether in the Hebrew, Greek, or English, is descriptive of our *churches* (plural), as opposed to *the Church* (or Body of Christ, the temple).

The northern tribes were called "the sons of Israel." Judah was a different entity, comprised of the southern tribes. The people in the southern kingdom were called "Jews"; and after the exile, they were called "The people of the Book." As noted before, the apostle Paul informs us:

But he is a Jew who is one inwardly; and circumcision is that which is of the heart, by the Spirit, not by the letter; and His praise is not from men, but from God (Romans 2:29).

According to Paul, it is a condition of the heart that designates whether or not one is a Jew, and circumcision represents the cutting away of the flesh. Paul taught that we are to die to the flesh—to crucify it because the flesh strives against the Spirit.

So here we are still. In Paul's day they were supposed to be moving into a deeper spiritual realm, just as today. But we, the Church (just like the early Church), have lagged behind, stumbling and dragging our feet in favor of the momentary satisfaction of the desires of the flesh.

Let's face it, our generation is made of consumers, and we are materialistic to the maximum! We have come to the place where we see this isn't "it," and we wonder, "Is this all there is?" We feel empty, lacking, and a bit frightened, but God is about to change everything!

Although we live in perilous times, we have things to do. We know that God is in control, and His eternal plan is moving forward. He continues to move us higher and higher, bringing us closer and closer to Him in His everlasting desire to fellowship with us and love us. He longs to speak to us through His Word, teaching us hidden truth—truth secretly hidden but whispered to us as we spend time with Him just as best friends always do.

Here is a little note from Him to you. It contains a few hints as to what we'll be doing together, in the very near future.

> *The afflicted and needy are seeking water, but there is none, and their tongue is parched with thirst; I, the Lord, will answer them Myself, as the God of Israel I will not forsake them. I will open rivers on the bare*

heights. And springs in the midst of the valleys; I will make the wilderness a pool of water, and the dry land fountains of water (Isaiah 41:17-18).

Arise, shine; for your light has come, and the glory of the Lord has risen upon you. For behold, darkness will cover the earth, and deep darkness the peoples; but the Lord will rise upon you, and His glory will appear upon you. And nations will come to your light (Isaiah 60:1-3a).

Listen! Your watchmen lift up their voices, they shout joyfully together; for they will see with their own eyes when the Lord restores Zion (Isaiah 52:8).

Sing to the Lord a new song, sing His praise from the end of the earth! You who go down to the sea, and all that is in it. You islands and those who dwell on them (Isaiah 42:10).

Go through, go through the gates; clear the way for the people; build up, build up the highway; remove the stones, lift up a standard over the peoples (Isaiah 62:10).

Lift up your eyes round about, and see; they all gather together, they come to you (Isaiah 60:4a).

For what had not been told them they will see, and what they had not heard, they will understand (Isaiah 52:15b).

…I will keep You and give You for a covenant of the people, to restore the land, to make them inherit the

desolate heritages; saying to those who are bound, "Go forth," and to those who are in darkness, "Show yourselves." Along the roads they will feed, and their pasture will be on all bare heights (Isaiah 49:8-9).

Come, Lord Jesus; "Thy kingdom come. Thy will be done, on earth as it is in heaven" (see Mt. 6:9-13).